A Cynic's Business Wisdom

A Cynic's Business Wisdom

Winning through Flexible Ethics

Jay J. Silverberg

So you may have a great education. So what? This is reality. Business is different out here.

Bruce McLean

BUSINESS EXPERT PRESS
Leader in applied, concise business books

A Cynic's Business Wisdom: Winning through Flexible Ethics
Copyright © Business Expert Press, LLC, 2021.

First published in 2021 by
Business Expert Press, LLC
222 East 46th Street, New York, NY 10017
www.businessexpertpress.com

ISBN-13: 978-1-95253-850-6 (paperback)
ISBN-13: 978-1-95253-851-3 (e-book)

Business Expert Press Entrepreneurship and Small Business Management Collection

Collection ISSN: 1946-5653 (print)
Collection ISSN: 1946-5661 (electronic)

Cover image licensed by Ingram Image, StockPhotoSecrets.com
Cover and interior design by S4Carlisle Publishing Services Private Ltd., Chennai, India

First edition: 2021

10 9 8 7 6 5 4 3 2 1

Printed in the United States of America.

Dedication

To my wife, Linda, and my three wonderful kids, Lauren, Noah, and Jonathan, who put up with my "inspired business craziness" for years, and thereafter, taught me, gently, how to enjoy the authentic fruits of life.

Abstract

The business universe is often characterized by its own rules, (purported) ethics, morals, scruples, intents and operating principals. While they are portrayed and taught as cast in stone, in reality, they are not. The key here is 'reality'. The real world of entrepreneurship revolves around 'survive-grow-adapt-succeed', and that absolutely gives the businessperson the opportunity to flex these norms to their own needs, always looking out for what is best for themselves. This book is intended to present, in an often edgy style, the 'how to' of taking care of number one, you, the entrepreneur.

Keywords

business ethics; ethics; flexible ethics; business; management; small business; entrepreneur; entrepreneurship; marketing; psychology of business; business hot buttons; getting to yes; success; success in business; real business; alternate business strategies; business rebel; leadership; business theatrics; business survival; communications; networking; branding; business health; business consultants; mentoring

Contents

Overture

You have to learn the rules of the game, and then you have to play better than anyone else.

Albert Einstein

A Cynic's Business Wisdom is an entrepreneur's survival manual from the edgy perspective that cynicism teaches us to have a healthy respect for the unknown and the unexpected. It equips us to effectively deal with real-world business challenges and capitalize on opportunities. After all, these are the cornerstones of being a businessperson.

This book personalizes business cynicism into a disarming and winning mindset for the entrepreneur. Each chapter also includes my personal experiences and business adventures in "This Is How It Works in Real Life."

It is a welcome respite for the battle-weary entrepreneur. It delivers deliciously digestible, unconventional, and sometimes eccentric tidbits of proven winning business tactics. I know. I've tried so very many of them myself.

This book responds to questions posed and issues raised by entrepreneurs, trainers, mentors, and businesspeople over my 20+ years delivering business consulting, and expounds on my advanced business workshops, as well as on my very own business ventures.

The book is a keen reflection of converting academic knowledge into unique workable business strategies, maneuvers, and techniques that promote growth and success.

Let's BBQ the Sacred Cow

Business is often not pretty. People are out to win at virtually any cost, especially your competitors. Hear those footsteps behind you? They are a constant reminder that you have a target on your back.

Business is not always "fair," played out on a level playing field. Life is not fair either. Get over it.

Flexible business ethics are part of empowering you with a highly competitive edge, learning to play by your rules and not those of everyone else. They are creative, edgy strategies and actions that are intended to give you an advantage in dealing with people, selling, networking, negotiating, and, most importantly, controlling every business situation you find yourself in.

Okay, let's play.

Business is actually quite simple. Cope, grow, succeed, trust nobody, look after yourself first, and have fun. The strategies in this book are uncommon, but highly effective. They may not always be what some might call "nice." However, they are legal, of course, and insightfully creative. Consider this survival manual as the flip side of all those "instant-gratification-sugar-coated-success-guaranteed-get-rich-overnight" books.

Once you recognize that business is a game, everyone is fundamentally selfish, nobody owes you a break, there are no black-and-white norms, only gray, and most of all, that business ethics are flexible, then you will understand how to play the game by your very own rules. This is a lot to absorb, I know.

George Burns is quoted as saying *"Authenticity is the key to winning. And if you can fake that, you've got it made."* That's flexible ethics in action.

This insightful Handbook is about the underbelly of business, the real world of clawing for a foothold, and, of course, winning. (This is a Handbook that cries out for a highlighter). These techniques will position you light-years ahead of your competition. Way ahead. And they work. Become a successful Business Rebel. I did it, and I won.

You Really Need to Know This

- How cynicism in business can instill a survival strategy
- How to play the game of business
- Advice from a unique perspective, and based on real-world experience, with lots of personal examples to learn from
- Entrepreneurship winning strategies not normally taught anywhere
- Cope–grow–succeed ideas based on my actual experience in the business world
- A novel approach to dealing with people, issues, and challenges

- "How-to" insight in dealing with (flexible) ethics, communications, self-promotion, the importance of being selfish, and capitalizing on the gray areas that inhabit the business world
- How best to gain the upper hand at every business encounter
- How to market and hit the clients'/customers' hot buttons that initiate sales using the art of persuasion
- Investment, partnerships, and funding advice, strategies, and warnings

Who Needs to Read This Handbook

- Business students, particularly upper level, including MBA, as well as advanced psychology, sociology, and management studies students
- Start-up and would-be entrepreneurs
- Established and experienced businesspeople
- Entrepreneurial trainers, mentors, professors, and consultants
- Sales and marketing professionals
- Business owners and managers
- Any professional involved in the psychology of business
- Academic professionals involved in business management

You have brains in your head.
You have feet in your shoes.
You can steer yourself any direction you choose.
You're on your own.
And you know what you know.
And you are the one who'll decide where to go.

Dr. Seuss

CHAPTER 1

What Is Business? It's Not Rocket Science

Business and financial intelligence are not picked up within the four walls of school. You pick them up in the streets. In school you are taught how to manage other people's money. On the streets you are taught how to make money.

Ajaero Tony Martins

Business is not easy, but it is not complicated either. It is an addictive "process" that needs to be followed in a logical sequence, one baby step at a time. It's also about street smarts, taking lessons from real life. There is an order and orderliness to it all.

Who Becomes an Entrepreneur, and Why?

Almost everyone dreams about it, many with fanciful sugar-plum stargazing. Countless try it. Far too few really succeed. Why? They just don't belong. It takes someone with the ability to thrive in this climate, yet naïve enough to not dwell on the pressures and roadblocks they will encounter.

There are four types of entrepreneurs that pretty well encompass all the stereotypes associated with businesspeople. Which one are you?

1. **The Opportunist** who spots a "can't lose" proposition and launches quickly into it. Research? Feasibility? Don't need them. Risk? Are you kidding me, this is a winner! Outcome? Generally disastrous.

2. **The Flyby** who acts out of jealousy (everyone is doing it, why not me?), misconception (being in business means huge income quickly), ignorance (it's easy), or complacency (sure, I'll give it a try). Also disastrous.

3. **The Deliberate Entrepreneur** who carefully researches and plans, creates Proformas without the use of rose-colored glasses, and slides into business rather than diving head first into the shallow end of the pool. I like this person.

4. **The Overthinker** characterized by someone who is working on the 10th+ version of a Business Plan, and whose friends are tired of being asked, "What do you think? Pretty good, huh?" I have no patience to keep validating the overthinker, other than being stupefied by their insecurities.

A Kid Started a Lemonade Stand

True story. A 10-year-old kid decided to open a lemonade stand. He was doing so to be able to buy a bike (goal). This is a business model for us all.

- The kid lived near a stop sign where there was steady walk-by traffic (location, location, location).
- He counted the cars, people, and joggers (market research).
- He asked his mom to help him buy the ingredients (supply chain).
- He worked out the cost per drink and what he thought he could charge (budgeting).
- He set up a stand and drew up a sign (marketing).
- He was polite and appreciative with all customers (customer service).
- He quit once he earned enough to buy a bike (exit strategy).

Seventeen Steps to Start a Business

1. Come up with an idea. This is the exciting part. You daydream about it.

2. Flesh out the idea, usually by endlessly babbling on to friends and business acquaintances. There should be a sparkle in your eyes. Check.

3. Write out your vision for the venture, how you see it. A little salivating is okay.

4. Set specific goals for yourself. What do you want out of the experience? Take off any rose-colored glasses when you do this.

5. Do your homework. Market research. Competition analysis. Wander somewhat aimlessly through others' similar ventures. When you're done, do more homework until you are sick of it and start seeing "commonalities" between businesses. Then stop.

6. Find a successful role model in your city, and pick their brains. Call them. Entrepreneurs are reclusive. They like to talk as long as they don't feel threatened. Be nice. Flatter. Be warm and fuzzy. Say nice things about them before you launch into your mini inquisition, for example, "Your website is awesome. It must really work for you."

7. Test your idea with people you trust. The keyword is "trust."

8. Do a "strengths, weaknesses, opportunities, threats/risks" analysis of your business.

9. How does the business fit your personality, skills, comfort level? Ask yourself. No fit? Don't do it.

10. Numbers crunching. Start-up budget. Break-even analysis. Cash flow. Now run it all again. Double your budgeted expenses and slash your revenues in half. Still profitable?

11. Do a Marketing Plan on how you will get to market, build awareness, and, yes, "steal" business from competition. After all, the market pie is finite. Someone will likely most begrudgingly give up some sales and clients to you. The more effective your Plan, the more you can appropriate.

12. Create an Operational Plan re location, traffic, and people to fill the skills you do not have or work you do not like. Boring, but necessary.

13. Create a Business Plan. Several actually, because the Plan needs to be tailored to the intended reader(s), that is, funders, investors, or for your own use. More or less graphical. More or less detailed, more or less salesy/promotional. See what I mean?

14. Create an Action Plan, namely, the baby steps you need to take to launch (or expand) your business. Milestones to reach and cross. These steps apply equally to those growing their businesses.

15. Take some acting classes. Seriously. Learn to communicate. Grasp the use of effective body language, and how to maintain a strong,

proactive image when meeting others. To many, this is almost play-acting, so learn to act. I am serious!

16. Money. Remember funders focus on "Protection of Capital, Profit (as in earning a bunch), and Exit Strategies." PPE (protection, profit, and exit). These are the three mantras of funders.

17. Ready to launch? One more thorough review. Anything change? Market shift? New competitors? Look around once more before taking the leap.

Stay hungry, and stay a little foolish.

Steven Paul

It's Business. It Breathes. It Changes. It's Alive!

There's nothing complacent about business. It's a living, breathing organism that reacts to everything around it: predators, markets, technology, trends and changing tastes, leapfrogging competition, wannabes, costs, currency markets, and even world events. You will be continually poked and prodded, and challenged. The business you have today is not the business it will be in 6, 12, or 24 months. Your sense of security and smugness may be short-lived. Complacency kills.

Change in business is a certainty. Weaponize this concept and make it a core strength of your business.

Change can impact any (or all) aspects of your business and it can be quite disruptive. Stay alert, stay aware, stay involved. For example, look at how major retailers have adapted to online shopping to deflect lower in-store sales and compete against the Amazons. Then look at the retailers who have shuttered their dinosaur retail stores because they did not change their core businesses.

Try to crystal ball when you can. Watch for trends. Join associations. Read trade magazines. Go to trade shows and industry conferences. Stay clued in, and current. Keep networking, and watch for new ideas, concepts, products, and services that can be "adapted" to your own business offerings.

Business Is Just Dealing with Businesspeople. Don't Overthink.

Business is "people to people." A building doesn't make decisions, nor does a corporate logo or a can of dog food. The people behind the product are the driving (or resistive) forces. Never lose sight of that perspective—it is a manager whom you are approaching in an effort to sell your wares, guided by corporate policy that dictates what they are supposed to accomplish, and what's in it for them. They simply do not account for the human element. Therein lies your penetration point.

When you are selling to Majorbigcorp, you are, in fact, selling only to the person who can buy from you, the person you meet, share some small talk, find out about their kids, show compassion (real or playacted) regarding their intense workload, and empathize with them re their cluttered desk. That's your client, not Majorbigcorp. Make them feel good … and important, even if they are not. They are your client.

Common Sense Is Not Very Common

Common sense is not universal. I would always intentionally design my marketing materials, websites, proposals, social media pages, and media articles to the lowest common denominator. Even in meetings, I would simplify my delivery so that nobody is "left behind." It's a safe bet that among the astute clients, contacts, and associates you deal with, that they also harbor some simpletons.

Compassion from Clients? Forget It!

Clients simply don't care. Got the sniffles? Having a bad day? Want to share it with the person you're having a meeting with? Don't share your "burden." It's yours, not theirs. Don't expect mommy to give you a cookie. Everybody has their own "baggage." Don't get caught in that "pity me–pity you" interchange.

Define What Business Is for You, and Only You

Business is personal. Everybody has their own aspirations, goalposts, and comfort zones. It is critical that your business fits your personality, your willingness to surrender personal freedom in exchange for downstream privilege, and your assurance to yourself and those who count on you, especially family, that you can do it. The mindset that you can succeed needs to be grounded in reality. You really don't want to scramble and stumble your way in a game of endless catch-up.

Create Something from Nothing, If You Can

Within reasonable bounds, you ask for the moon, you go a little crazy,
and you let the excitement of it all be your impetus to succeed.

Jay J. Silverberg

You go into business because an idea or opportunity excites and motivates you. That idea could have been generated by virtually anything, anywhere, anytime, and there is no shortage of stimuli. There are three basic genres of new venture creation.

1. **Copycat** an existing product or service. This is likely the most common business launch. You see a place in the market, or feel that you can do something better. This is the least risky avenue since others already serve an existing market, and your goal is to carve a piece for yourself.
2. **Filling a void** takes copycat one step further insofar as you identify a void within an existing market. Maybe an add-on product or service. Again, this is a reasonably sound and safe approach. You are coat tailing or improving something already out there.
3. **Creating something from nothing** is the most challenging and usually the most profitable and exhilarating business creation pathway. In modern times, Apple has reinvented creating something from nothing. Did we know we couldn't live without iPods, iPads, or sexy cell phones? Someone had to tell us, and it was Steve Jobs. Wherever you see an opportunity to launch something innovative and edgy, think seriously about it. It is electrifying. It can be risky and expensive and may require a strategic partner or investor, but don't shun it because it scares you, or you are uncertain you can rise to

the challenge. You probably can, you know. (However, if it really terrifies you, walk away). So, who told you that you needed Red Bull super-caffeinated energy drink?

This Is How It Works in Real Life

Here's an example of creating something from nothing.

Early on in my "entrepreneur-dom," I designed and built a multimillion dollar plant to produce non-nutritive cellulose flour, finely ground sawdust that was used as a filler in foods, pharmaceuticals and cosmetics. Since you may have inadvertently eaten some of my sawdust product, I beg your forgiveness. But, it was probably healthy for you. Extra fiber. Anyways, I planned that venture on the back of a napkin in a restaurant. It was a euphoric experience, that is, until the million red flags popped up. They were called "common sense," including the fact that there was a recession and I was looking to create a new business venture for myself that had "legs."

With some research, I identified a large U.S.-based company whom I knew needed the commodities I was going to produce. Their procurement people confirmed their supply shortfall.

I needed engineering expertise so I hired the engineering team who serviced the multinational client I wanted to pursue as a core customer and drafted some preliminary facility specs and costs.

I then approached the prospective client and asked for a standing order, in writing, for everything I could produce, and several million dollars to build the facility. They actually laughed about the funding, but, to my delight and astonishment, they did give me a multiyear purchase order. That was all I needed to secure venture capital.

In essence, I recognized the need for "common sense" once the honeymoon of germinating the idea on a napkin had worn thin. I surrounded myself with good support people. I concealed my apprehension. I secured financing, engineering know-how, and then built and ran the plant. I succeeded. What a ride!

Sometimes a smattering of naivety helps, too. So don't let anyone tell you that you shouldn't try. It's your business dream.

CHAPTER 2

Business Is a Game

Think of business as a game. Lots of competition and a minimum of rules.

Bill Gates

Business is often referred to as a "game," complete with competition, rules, penalties, and rewards, quite analogous to a sports event. In fact, there are even a number of board games that have business as a central theme, including Monopoly. Online games abound that correlate business to games or competitions. Simulation games such as "Game Corp," "Frontier," "Burger Restaurant," "Stock-o-Mania," and "Shop Empire" are just a few that are designed for all age groups, from kids to teens and right up to university students.

Unlike board games played with good humor at the kitchen table, business is a game to the death; often financial death, anyway! It is also a game that can represent large piles of money—your money.

The successful entrepreneurs, who experience the absolute exhilaration of "scoring," pride themselves on understanding the game and how to use the system to their ultimate advantage. Luck has little to do with success, unless you are fortunate enough to be born with, or marry into, money. Being able to recognize that you are in the right place at the right time is also sometimes called "luck," but it's really business savvy.

Want to Be a Successful Businessperson?

You don't have to be a superhuman from Planet Krypton or an incurable gambler. You don't have to possess the lightning reactions and lust for victory of a Formula 1 driver or the IQ of Albert Einstein.

Although the merits of the products or services involved in the business venture are important, they are actually less significant than you might imagine. What counts most, aside from your improvisatory and innovative skills, as well as your ability to "deliver the goods," is how well you play the game, how well you promote your business and yourself, and if you truly have the motivation, drive, and psychological makeup of the true, die-hard entrepreneur. To achieve this, you must also arm yourself with a keen knowledge of whatever business "nasties" can, and will, come your way.

You have to be a creative, innovative visionary with loads of staying power. You should not only fully understand the intricacies of the business world, but also be able to act instinctively and "play" any situation to your ultimate benefit. Puritanical business ideals and inflexibly high standards of conscience are definitely not assets.

The first rule of every game is to know you are in one.

Sandy Lerner

You must be aware of the "game" and what it takes to survive and win. In the game of business, one should understand right away that the rules are flexible. Sometimes you will find yourself wondering if everyone else is even playing by whatever rules there are. You will find yourself in a cold world of playacting, gutter wars, flank protection, and zero tolerance for the hesitant. Don't blink or forget to duck. Maintain a high level of peripheral vision. Don't allow yourself to get fat or content. A squad of lean and hungry players is waiting to snatch the business dice from your hands. Forewarned is indeed forearmed.

Children Play Business Games Too

Business as a competitive sport is promoted from early childhood on, until the opportunity to participate in the "real business world" presents itself. There are a number of children's games that are based on entrepreneurship, such as Children's Business[1] and the interactive website Biz Kids,[2] which teaches young entrepreneurs how to start and run a business. There are also a host of organizations such as the 4H Club that promote leadership and management. Even The Boy Scouts offer badges for business merit and entrepreneurship and encourage a competitive and winning spirit.

Business Is Just a Sports Event

The similarities between business and competitive sports abound. Here are just a few:

- Your Business Plan is a playbook.
- Your brand/logo is your team crest.
- Your mentor is your coach.
- You gain confidence by scoring, winning.
- Promoting yourself and building your image in public is called "marketing," same as any ball player or ball club.
- Your risks, instead of physical, are personal and financial.
- Your fan base is your loyal client base.

Calculated Risk-Taking, Not Crapshoots

Every decision involved in going into, surviving in, and expanding a business implies risk-taking, to varying degrees. It is up to you to develop the skill of "calculated risks" and avoid the go-for-broke, blind crapshoots. Selective risk allows you to stack the deck in your favor as much as possible, and even then, although the outcome is not predictable, your chances for achieving desirable results will be much greater than leaving it up to luck alone. Make your own luck wherever possible.

---

[1]Children's Business. 2017. https://boardgamegeek.com/boardgame/170179/childrens-business, (date accessed June 10, 2020).

[2]Biz Kids. http://bizkids.com/, (date accessed June 10, 2020).

- Remember, every move costs not only money, but time, and the implications also include your health, personal life, friends, and family. Only you can properly judge what you can afford to risk or lose.
- Your gut feel instincts got you where you are now. Don't discard them.
- Risk is a very personal issue. Everybody sets their own level of acceptability and should live comfortably within those boundaries.
- Never mortgage the house, kids, cars, and mother-in-law, or deplete your lifesavings for a business. No business is worth gambling your entire portfolio, regardless of the risk factor. Your security, in its entirety, is too precious to put on the line.
- Using "Other People's Money" (known as "OPM") is better than your own.
- "Get rich quick schemes" aren't. Do not fall for the oversell and pressure tactics. Search out the flaws and question everything. Remember, if it's such an extraordinary moneymaking venture, why are they sharing it with you? I certainly wouldn't.
- Avoid investing or going into business with friends or family. Any problems that arise will strain or even destroy the relationship.
- Measure every move in terms of personal values, and ask yourself if it is all worth it.
- The opportunity that has a short time span to respond to, should probably not be acted upon, unless you are very familiar with all the aspects of the proposition. Don't let time, or the lack thereof, be the major deciding factor.
- Avoid increasing your fixed overheads in "anticipation" of more business, but rather as it materializes. Don't get ahead of yourself.
- When a decision in your business demands some corrective action, choose the one that has the least permanent fallout and not necessarily the one that costs the least.
- Above all, be guided by what you are comfortable with. The nature of business itself demands that you take certain risks, push farther, and stretch yourself to your limits and beyond. Do only what is "right" for you.

Winning at Business Is Very Personal

Every entrepreneur needs to set their own targets for success.

- What is your definition of success?
- How far do you want to take your entrepreneurial experience?
- When is enough considered enough?
- What are you trying to achieve from a personal growth aspect? Financial growth?
- How much risk are you comfortable taking?
- Are you driven by your own version of success and at ease in stressful situations that may arise?

So, Let the Game Begin

All games have hunters and the hunted. Which one are you?

If all would-be entrepreneurs fully comprehended what they were getting themselves into, they would probably seek employment with regular pay checks, vacations, security, fixed working hours, and indexed pension plans complete with health plans. These perks do not characterize the world of the entrepreneur. Financial feast and famine are often more typical of the early years of growing a business.

On the other hand, the rewards of building a successful business are virtually unparalleled. The feelings of accomplishment and recognition are indescribable, as are independence and the pursuit of monetary gains. This is a magnificent high.

This Is How It Works in Real Life

I had developed some sophisticated economic modeling to measure a community's ability to survive and grow in any economic sector, particularly after a major event such as the shutdown of a key community employer. The modeling was successfully used by various government ministries as part of their planning processes.

A business friend pointed out to me that a (much loathed) competitor included my proprietary model in one of his reports and claimed it as his own. It was verbatim from my website.

I then proceeded to post fictitious and outrageously extravagant economic data on my website, citing work utilizing my model. Sure enough, this soon appeared in the competitor's next report, and he was mercilessly lambasted by the client. I discreetly deleted the false data from my website, and, incidentally, we won the next three contracts.

My competitor's company was actually sound, but the owner often exhibited loose morals, beyond flexible ethics.

Trust nobody. Know your audience. Know your competition. Do just about anything (legal) to win.

Impish is okay too.

CHAPTER 3

Be a Business Rebel

There is only one way to avoid criticism—do nothing, say nothing and be nothing.

Aristotle

Being a Business Rebel is all part of adopting flexible ethics.

The Business Rebel employs tactics nobody ever teaches in school. Edgy perspectives and advice that come from winning (and occasionally losing, but still learning) from business. Building successful businesses, and taking a few hits along the way, will give you a perspective that no amount of academic teachings can compete with.

Winners recognize that playing by the rules won't get you what you want.

Losers get in line to chase and drool over those more successful, while being hunted like quarry by those jealously trailing them. Not a pretty image, right?

What Are the Character Strengths of a Business Rebel?

A Business Rebel stops following staid business rules, and certainly stops tailgating competitors who are likely crowding the marketplace. None of us can keep doing business the old school way where we fall in line and become an "also-ran." It's far too congested out there.

A Rebel takes the "I am not a sheep" approach and does the unexpected. People remember them.

A Rebel is an innovator, unafraid to try new strategies like offbeat guerilla marketing or taking chances somewhat beyond the norm. Being less orthodox is key.

A Rebel is a fighter and leader who fears conformity and is not a follower.

Super-rebels like Steve Jobs and Elon Musk, for example, who, themselves, become a "brand."

Business Rebel Tactics They Won't Teach You, but I Will

Having started and run six successful companies and helped a multitude of businesspeople with entrepreneurial training and mentoring, I have learned a number of "real-world how-to" business strategies that really work, the kind of stuff they never seem to teach you in school or other business programs. A number of these are covered in separate chapters in this how-to book, but here is a "fifty-thousand-foot overview" of some of the key tactics (they are called "tactics" because, well, business is a game of combat).

> *Do today what others won't, so tomorrow you can do what others can't.*
>
> Jerry Rice

- Be unpredictable. Develop an attitude. Make people smile, and comfortable, because that is when they are most vulnerable.
- Gain a following, a fan club. Stand out. Stand apart. Dare to be different.
- Leapfrog challengers. Leave others choking on your dust.
- Do only what's good for you, not just what might be expected from you. Every decision, every idea, and everything you do needs to be beneficial to number 1—you, and only you.
- Attract attention; become memorable to your client/customer base.
- Understand what drives your market, and become a driver (not a passenger).
- By being somewhat rebellious, customers feel rebellious dealing with you. That's a good thing.
- Learn about the "hot buttons" to push to get customers/clients to say "yes," and feel good about it, too.

- Wield sales-closing power when you recognize others' greed, ego, pride, and sloth as motivators.
- Recognize other peoples' "selfish gene." It's human nature that everyone acts out of their own self-interest. Learn how to manipulate it to get others to give you what you want.
- Are you a boring businessperson? Get unboring by repackaging yourself, your company, your brand, and even your personality, and watch what happens!
- Playact your business role. It's part of the game of business. Become someone customers are happy to deal with and competitors are insecure about.
- Be passionate about what you do. This will carry you far when the going gets tough.
- Keep it simple. Don't try to market or sell tons of products or services. Try to focus on one revenue stream, and make it work before you expand your offerings.
- Shorten the steps to generating revenue. Revenue and business cash flow are key.
- When planning a project or business of any kind, the more people you need to "bring to the table," the less chance of it all happening.
- Every cent you spend should go toward generating revenue. Forget fancy offices and new cars. Conserving cash is essential.
- Take part in a large market. That makes it easier to capture a portion of it.
- Profit and the bottom line are of paramount importance. Yes, there is satisfaction and freedom to set your hours and lifestyle. But most importantly, earning a profit in your business buys you the privilege of enjoying all the other perks.
- Don't ask your mother, sisters, or brothers if your business idea makes sense to them. They will say "of course" because they love you, or "don't be ridiculous" because they may be jealous.
- Before you take on a partner, think about what you want them to bring to the business, besides money. Sales contacts? Business experience? Choose a partner carefully. Remember your friend who spent years trying to get out of a marriage? Partnership breakups can be worse.
- "Reach out" for business. It won't come to you.

- If you are digging yourself into a hole, stop digging! Figure out why and how to change things.
- Enjoy your successes, but don't take them for granted.
- Keep moving.

Even More Winning Business Rebel Tactics

Nobody said being a Business Rebel was easy, but, frankly, the experience of being the renegade, and winning by doing so, is exhilarating. Getting comfortable with these additional tactics is important for entrepreneurs.

- Never argue with a customer. You cannot ever win. Work to find a trade-off where both parties can accept the outcome without losing too much "face" or pride.
- You will have clients you do not like. There will be personality clashes. Learn to get past those and focus on the business at hand.
- Compliment others, even where those compliments may not be even remotely sincere. Ego is a major "hot button" in building relationships and winning customers. Dislike their website? Appalled by their language? Get over it. Suck it up.
- Put up a good front image. That includes great business cards, website, promotional material and social media. Winners like dealing with winners. Even if you are a start-up, make sure your image is rock solid.
- Stay confident. There will be situations where customers will put you on the spot, on the hot seat. They may question your experience, or possibly your pricing structure. This is only a test. Stay in character, that is, always maintain the strong and confident character that you want them to see.
- Small talk is often painful, but is a necessary part of the "courting ritual" between you and your customers. Find common ground like family or sports. But avoid anything to do with politics and religion, diet or exercise.
- Never complain, or tell others you are feeling ill, have a cold, or a sore shoulder. Everyone has "baggage," and sharing yours does nothing to build a relationship. It is not a bonding experience.

- There will be surprises that crop up. Don't look or act surprised. Deal with the challenge. Pretend to deflect it.
- It is okay to talk about yourself, and your abilities, but not before your customer has a chance to talk about themselves and their needs. Listening is critical and allows you time to formulate a response that will be well received. And as for "bragging" about yourself, a little goes a long way.
- Keep the "What's in it for me" (WIIFM) thinking in mind, and zero in not on what you can deliver, but instead what you can provide that will meet the customer's needs, make their job (or life) easier, give them more free time, or simply more profit.
- Never burn bridges with people, no matter how tempted you are to do so. You never know when you might need to cross that bridge in the future.
- In Hollywood, there used to be a cliché "Never let them see you cry." The same applies in business. Don't share disappointments as it does not earn you much respect.

Disrupt the Competition

You're never too young to dream big.

Bansky

The danger in being (or becoming) a Business Rebel is that you may overstep and become outrageous or scandalous. Being a rascal is fine. Becoming an outrageous outcast is self-defeating. The objective is to disrupt the competition. So choose your tactics carefully. Your industry and marketplace may be more amenable to a rebellious approach, or it might be so staid that adopting rebel strategies needs to be done with some care. How much can the marketplace react positively to? Test it out.

What Type of Business Rebel Are You?

Reflect on who you are and how you are perceived. Then change it to become more of an attention-getter. Find the spotlight that works.

There are four distinct types of rebels. Which one are you, or could you become?

1. The **"traveler"** enjoys diversity, meeting new people, exploring, sharing, and rebels against conformity.
2. The **"climber"** seeks new perspectives and has a penchant for novelty.
3. The **"pirate,"** as the name implies, is a fearless explorer and adventurer.
4. The **"guard"** believes in order, conformity, stability, and tradition as the cornerstones to succeed.

The climber and the pirate are today's trademark rebels and business heroes, for example, Musk, Zuckerberg and Bezos.

Being a Business Rebel requires a degree of self-reflection and adaptation. Choose what works for you and your marketplace, and then take it just a smidgen further. (That's what I would be, but then again, I *AM* a Business Rebel.)

This Is How It Works in Real Life

I was approached by a community that had a once beautiful marine park called "Seal Bay." While it was still a natural congregating spot for basking seals and sea lions, the regional government committed no funds to its upkeep and the park became a party spot. The litter and damage was shameful and the unchecked vegetation was overtaking the park's natural beauty. The Seal Bay Citizens Group asked for my help.

With no money available, my strategy was to draw attention to Seal Bay. I put an ad in the local newspaper "Seal Bay Condominium Project. Thirty new waterfront condos and marina. Tennis courts. RV parking." The community residents took notice, but no amount of complaining by them to the regional government proved effective.

I placed a second story that an aquarium had agreed to come and collect all the seals and sea lions, much beloved by the residents, and cart them away. That was the breaking point. Even after it was revealed that the Seal Bay stories and condo project were hoaxes, the park received the attention it deserved. Seal Bay was funded and restored, and it still continues as a natural wildlife sanctuary and park.

Of course, I had angered the regional government stakeholders. To win their "affection," I assisted them to market Seal Bay as a tourist attraction, so that relationship was salvaged. Win–win–win.

CHAPTER 4

Business Is Inspired Craziness

If you are not willing to risk the usual, you will have to settle for the ordinary.

Jim Rohn

There is something very unnatural and frightening about the entrepreneurial process, especially when the individual is "possessed" with the affliction to "make it happen." To watch a serious business being planned and built, it becomes clearly evident to the observer that this is not a whim or spur-of-the-moment decision. Nobody, sane or otherwise, gets up in the morning, stretches the sleep from their tired body, and declares "Today I will become a self-employed workaholic."

Rather, it is an obsession that has gradually been generated by a series of factors that have affected your life, decisions mulled over and taken, events that have shaped your outlook and your goals, and a strong element of drive and determination implanted firmly somewhere in your brain that controls your destiny. (It is my firm belief that the parts of a person's brain that lead them to become "born-again" entrepreneurs are inextricably linked to their pleasure and pain centers, from button-bursting pride to masochism, and all ports of call in between). There is absolutely nothing wrong with the excitement and kinetic forces that drive the entrepreneur, and if tempered with a smidgen of realism and a planned approach, you have an excellent chance at succeeding.

"Inspired Craziness" dictates that your ideas, as offbeat as they may seem to you at first, or to others, are worthy of the rationalization process that will lead to one of three outcomes: abandon the concept and take a vacation, modify your ideas to make them workable, or prove their validity. The latter two lead to a business.

Don't limit your imagination or automatically discard a concept that came from left field, or because someone else, no matter who, says it cannot be done. Great business people use other's negative feedback as an impetus to succeed, while subconsciously taking heed of those very same commentaries.

Every business notion that you generate is an inspiration, and should be respected accordingly. Once conceived, give your imagination the freedom to explore. It is far easier to discard unworkable options during the ongoing planning process and thereby allowing sufficient time to consider alternatives.

However, the "raison d'être" of you going into business is also important. Too many people venture into business on false premises or for reasons that lead to certain self-destruction. A few such scenarios of true craziness that I have witnessed are worthy of exploration.

Misguided Visions?

God never told you to go into business. He didn't speak to you directly, or even through a burning bush. Neither your goldfish nor your two month old toddler whispered secrets to you. Your hazy dream of a vision was probably heartburn or will become so if you try to build a business around a misguided notion. There are enough "mixed nuts" out there in the business world already—just pick up a franchise handbook and read about customized coffin liners or tree surgery made easy.

Greed?

This is not to be confused with ambition, which is a viable driving force. Greed is a blinding, debilitating motive that, best case, will cause you to greatly overestimate your potential, thereby crippling your chances right from the beginning. Worst case, it leads you directly into the clutches of fast-buck artists or get-rich-quick schemers, most of whom abandon ethics in general, and prey on the weak, vulnerable, and gullible.

Ego and Pride?

You want to go into business because you know you are terrific and can do it? Don't quit your day job. If your ego is greater than your ideas or ability to perform, then you are likely being blinded by false images. That is why it is important to seek out valued contacts with whom to discuss your concepts. While not necessarily heeding all their advice, at least you get a sounding board. Pride, on the other hand, as a kissing cousin to ego, is a crucial factor in your mental makeup and contributes to the confidence you must steadfastly maintain in yourself and your venture.

"I'm Smarter than My Peers"

If the people you work with or the management that employs you is, by your very own standards, slower off the mark than you feel you are, you may just be working at a stupid company. This is not necessarily indicative of the entire business world, so look around carefully before making the leap.

"The System Owes Me"

Okay, you've put in your time as manager, accounts receivable, letters "a" through "f" at Acme Dumplings and Sweetrolls, Inc. That alone, or that as a major deciding factor, hardly qualifies you for the honor of entrepreneurship. Furthermore, simply because you have paid loads of taxes over a number of years, or have been unhappy at a series of jobs, doesn't represent a reason to go into business for yourself. In fact, with that kind of an attitude, you are probably too "angry" to even consider the grueling challenge of self-employment, and any idea that you may generate in your present mindset will be deemed as fantastic, regardless of merit ... full steam ahead, blind and oblivious to the rigors and pitfalls that await you.

The System Owes You Nothing

Zilch. In fact, nobody owes you anything, except that you do owe yourself the opportunity to explore business possibilities in a more rational framework, free of any grudges or misconceptions about entitlement or the system being obligated to you, or the perception that "now it's your turn." Don't waste your time. Go fishing and recharge your batteries instead.

Doing This for the Family?

Today's semi-rigid social structure dictates that you work to better your family, to provide more vacations, bigger homes, fancier gas-guzzlers, and more sophisticated toys. Not for yourself, but for your own little "tribe." While the sentiment is admirable and the resulting benefits for your family are, more often than not, appreciated, do not fool yourself. How does quitting your job and risking not only your financial resources but also your future lifestyle, correlate to providing security for your family? Yes, possibly down the road, once you have made it, but how about the shaky, early transitional period laden with risks and hurdles?

Everything you do is inherently selfish. When you give to a charity, you do it because it makes you feel good about yourself, and lucky that nobody you know is in as sorry a state as the poor soul depicted in the "Save Africa" television ad. When you help your kids, you feel useful and as wise as a sage, and when you help your 86-year-old Aunt Martha buy a new wheelchair, you praise the Lord that you are not that old and senile yet.

When you go into business for yourself, you do it for you, first and foremost. Be selfish. If others around you benefit from your efforts, that's a rewarding secondary effect. Don't dupe yourself and others to the contrary, and don't go into business for everybody or anybody else except yourself. Martyrdom is not fashionable in the business milieu.

A Better Mousetrap

I have witnessed, far too often, whereby inventors who, totally oblivious to the state of the art around them, or worse, in total disregard to market needs, launched businesses and invested time and money around a product or service that will never, ever fly. For example, "Here, look it works, and I can sell it for $249." "Yes, but who would want one?" Dead end.

It Looks Easy

If that is the case, you haven't done your homework. This naïve outlook is the result of inadequate planning and brainstorming on all the "what-ifs" that affect any business. If your would-be competitor makes it look easy, then study them to see what they are doing right (and what they are avoiding).

If you go into business with the idea that you will put your competitor into bankruptcy in short-order, then you had better be prepared to meet your competition at your own bankruptcy hearing. They will be there to pick up the pieces, if you have anything left.

Inspired craziness is steeped in commitment and is judiciously meticulous in planning and control. It is a mixed marriage of zeal and prudence. It does not command blind faith.

If we want to achieve greatness, stop asking for permission.

Eddie Colla

This Is How It Works in Real Life

I once had a multinational client who produced and distributed liquid nitrogen, mostly for the food and pharmaceutical industries. My role was to work with anyone who approached the company with new freezing applications that had potential for commercialization that could benefit my client.

On one occasion, I took a meeting with an inventor who claimed to have spent years in India perfecting a new "aphrodisiac" product that required liquid nitrogen freezing. I was skeptical, but kind of curious (and amused) too. He arrived at my office, disheveled, carrying a small beer cooler, apparently with samples.

As it turned out, his new product was ground up frozen tiger testicles. I commiserated with the tigers. After politely dismissing him, I realized that he had shared with me his inspired craziness, regardless of his bizarre entrepreneurial path. This was his dream, eccentric that it might be.

I still sided with the tigers.

CHAPTER 5

The Glorified Image of Being Self-Employed

Don't go around saying the world owes you a living. It was here first.
Mark Twain

When people fall in love, it is forever, totally mutual and the best ever, each and every time they fall in love. Being self-employed is embodied by the same spirit. It is worshiped by those who dream about it, lauded by those who are in business, and hyped by those charlatans who sell "instant riches" to the gullible uninitiated.

The entrepreneurial world is an enriching, exciting, vibrant environment for those who are ready. However, it is not the fabled garden of paradise either, as those who hawk business opportunities would have you believe.

Entrepreneurship is neither painless nor Hollywood-style glamorous. The hours are never-ending, the money is often sporadic at first, the security is what you make it, and the longevity of your venture is dependent on your staying power.

Your "Aha" Moment

That's when everything you have been thinking about, planning, dreaming, venting, sleeping fitfully, and distracted by suddenly comes together. It is defined as "a moment of sudden insight or discovery."

It suddenly makes sense. You realize what you need to do, and how to do it. You have gotten your arms around the entrepreneurial beast, and you start (or are ready) to move forward. That goes hand in hand with the

"**WOW**" factor, when you understand the scope of your business venture and, frankly, you impress yourself. That's a good thing.

This is not only for new start-ups. It applies equally to established businesses that are growing, or changing in an ever-changing market-place, or reacting to competition. And in doing all of this, there are two other acronyms to remember.

1. "**MACS**" means you should be undertaking this with "massive amounts of common sense."
2. "**MYTOP**" means "multiply yourself through other people." In other words, surround yourself with those you trust, and bounce your ideas off them. (But not friends or family, because they will likely only tell you what you want to hear.)

Entrepreneur's Self-Assessment Checklist. How Do You Stack Up?

Here is a checklist for wannabes and newbies as well as established entrepreneurs reexamining their entrepreneurial path. There are no right or wrong answers, but the results will shed some light on your fitness and ability to survive and thrive in business.

Ask Yourself
Are you hardworking?
Do you stay focused on a project you are working on?
Do you have a spirit of adventure?
Are you persistent? Stubborn?
Do you get along well with others?
Are you a risk-taker? Calculated risk-taker? Cautious and conservative?
When you decide to do something, do you need to finish it?
When you begin a task, do you set out goals? Steps to succeed?
Do you tackle and solve problems?
When people tell you it can't be done, do you still find a way to do it?
Do you get personal satisfaction doing and completing a good job?
Do you consider yourself a leader, or a follower?
Do you need others to tell you that you are doing a good job?

Do you avoid difficult or confrontational situations?
Are you a good "loser" or a sore "loser" in competitive situations?
Do you seek advice from people?
How do you deal with negative feedback from someone?
Do you feel good about yourself?
Do you like being in charge of other people?
Do you usually come up with more than one solution to a problem?
Do you find it easy to get others to do something for you?
Are you constantly thinking of new ideas? Projects?
Do you like to take care of details?
Do you get bored easily?
What rates higher: personal satisfaction or money?
Do you enjoy socializing, meeting people?
Do you believe in "good luck," or creating your own luck?
Do you take rejection personally?
Do you wake up happy most of the time?
When you get an idea stuck in your head, do you constantly play it over and over?
Do you believe entrepreneurship needs to be a huge risk?
Can you accept resignation without admitting defeat?
Do you learn from your mistakes?
How quickly do problems frustrate you?
Do you find change difficult, fun, or challenging?
Are you a good listener?
Advice? Do you look for someone to agree with you?

To be successful you must act big, think big, talk big.

Aristotle Onassis

Promise Yourself

- Allow yourself to dream.
- Set goals you can reach, but only if you "stretch."
- Understand that business is a moving target.
- If your gut feel is screaming, or whispering to you, listen to it.
- Accept that you are a bit crazy.
- You are different. Don't apologize.

- Only you can set your limitations.
- Be fashionably rebellious.
- Stay proactive, out there.
- Accept that "what's in it for me" means you first.
- Get comfortable playacting your business persona.
- Expect no gifts as there will be none forthcoming.
- Learn to listen.
- Practice communicating and networking. They are learned skills.
- Adopt "flexible ethics" in everything you do.
- Don't underprice or undersell yourself.
- Find a way. There is always a way.
- Live up to promises, to yourself and to others.
- Never let them see you cry.
- Don't be afraid to ask for business, or money.

Why Are You an Entrepreneur?

I have a new address. I'm living outside my comfort zone.

Brett Hoebel

Ask yourself why you are on this entrepreneur joyride. Bored? Frustrated? Eager to change? Enjoy mountain climbing, caving, or shark cage diving, because being in business offers similar adrenaline rushes? Your dog or canary whispers encouragement to you? When you gamble, do you play the 25-cent slots or the $500 blackjack tables?

But seriously, you need to take a step back and ask yourself why exactly you are in business, and what you realistically expect to get out of it. And what is your risk tolerance level? Do you have life goals you cannot achieve through a 9-to-5 job?

Are you a leader, or a sheep? Can you wallow in failure as much as delight in success?

Are you thin-skinned, retreating from assaults that offend your precious feelings or invade your "space"?

Regardless, the best way to predict your future is to create it.

This Is How It Works in Real Life

When I started my consulting business, someone directed me to a marketing guru, let's call him Dirk. He had built a solid business with a lot of multinational clients, and I fully expected him to supply me with some leads and open a few doors since I had been referred by a mutual friend.

Well, we had a nice chat and I got some fatherly advice, but that was all. Two years later, Dirk called me up to see if I was still in business. Astonished, I replied "certainly" (but held back adding "but no thanks to you"). He had some business to pass my way, but, before doing so, he wanted to make sure I had the staying power before putting his "arrogant self" on the line with his clients.

Don't expect gifts. Nobody gives you anything just because you happen to need it now.

CHAPTER 6

Flexible Business Ethics

Do one thing every day that scares you.

Eleanor Roosevelt

So, What Exactly Are Flexible Business Ethics?

They represent strategies, actions, and attitudes that deliver results and rewards for you and your business. Flexing gives you an edge to win at almost (I said "almost") any cost. It is legal. It is not intended to harm, but the tactics may be borderline socially acceptable. Flexible business ethics action can include the following, to varying degrees:

- Manipulation
- Coercion
- Pretense
- Feigning interest or knowledge
- Adaptation to unfamiliar situations
- Anything outside your comfort zone that requires "faking it"

Flexible business ethics means bending the rules for gaining advantage, but nothing illegal, offensively immoral, terribly damaging, misguidedly ego-driven, malicious, or narcissistic. Other than that, anything goes.

Some businesspeople consider settling for gray borders that extend the flexible ethics definition to lying, stealing, and cheating. Avoid any such temptation. It exacts a price.

Think in Shades of Gray in a Black-and-White World

There are no hard-and-fast rules for business ethics because people's actions and decisions are dictated on decidedly more personal, corporate, and career motivational factors.

The business milieu, with its codes of behavior and performance, is generally perceived in hard-edged black-and-white terms. That's definitely wrong, and you had better realize that from the onset. The entire business spectrum represents limitless degrees of concessions and compromise— the very cornerstones of flexible ethics. The process of bending (but not fracturing) the rules is continuously colored by an entrepreneur's survival instincts and drive to succeed.

Be prepared to, sometimes, swallow your pride for the sake of a sale, delivering disingenuous flattery, exhibiting false humility, and playacting someone to project an alter-image that the client needs to see. It's all part of becoming a business chameleon. Flexible ethics are tools that serve you well.

Examples of Flexible Business Ethics. Try Some On.

I knew all the rules, but the rules did not know me.

Eddie Vedder

- Smiling and acting friendly with someone who is detestable, but whose business you want.
- Aggrandizing your experience and abilities. Boasting shamelessly.
- Enhancing your website and social media pages, plunging your toe into fantasy territory.
- Forced flattery. "I really like your (whatever). Really I do!"
- Taking on a questionable contract or work based moreso on your cash flow needs.
- Playing "takeaway" (pretending to walk away from business), in hopes of the client agreeing to your prices, all-the-while hungering for their business.
- Smiling and joking all the way through sales negotiations/meetings with the owner's obnoxious, boring, and brain-dead nephew.

- Using people as stepping stones to get to others (covered in greater detail later).
- Adopt a business personality far removed from your own, and likely outside your comfort zone.
- Bogus sincerity. "I'm sorry to hear that. I understand how you feel."
- Find a cause or charity for your company to support, based solely on what it can do for your public image. It's not the "cause," it's the PR that comes with supporting it.
- Package yourself personally to boost yourself (and your company) in others' eyes.
- Name-drop. Nobody really ever checks.
- Practice selective perception. Hear only what you want to or need to.
- Playact sincerity and empathy for others, as well as humility. Pretending can earn you brownie points.
- Adopt your clients' causes and passions. Greenie? Sports crazy? Music lover? That's me too!
- Feel like a star. Be a star. Act like a winner. Always.
- Don't ever let your guard down; it exposes your weaknesses.
- Never complain. Nobody cares. Seriously.

Think how some of these apply to you. Practice. Learn to use them to your maximum advantage.

Business Ethics Have Little to Do with Business

This section is definitely a portrayal about the darker side of business, beyond acceptable limits. You need to be very aware of it for your own well-being.

Business ethics are often a cover for businesspeople to do unethical things. The phrase is as much a contradictory mismatch (oxymoron) as "military intelligence," "happy birthday," "jumbo shrimp," or "progressive conservative." Businesspeople set their own codes of behavior and ethics, based on five simple principles:

1. What they, themselves, and their business may need or want in order to succeed and to fulfill their own needs.

2. Logic, in terms of how to carry out their plans that benefit only them.

3. Socially acceptable behavior, thereby normally limiting their actions to within the boundaries of the law. This does not preclude bending the outer edges.

4. What they feel they can get away with and still remain a player within their designated field of commerce. If they are powerful, there are few boundaries. If they are new to the game, the allowable risks are of a lesser magnitude and potentially less detrimental to their position in the market.

5. Poker-style bluffing, skating, that is, the art of not responding directly, and other immensely useful strategies to be discussed in detail later.

A certain darkness is needed to see the stars.

Osho

The PYA Doctrine Exemplifies Flexible Business Ethics

Everyone who is in business looks out for "number 1," or they really should be. The employee, at any level, in any size company, from secretary to vice president, is governed by the "Protect Your A**" (PYA) principle. If your firm can enhance a managers' position for advancement by offering them "brownie points", then you will be well received.

If, on the other hand, you represent a challenge and threat to their authority and livelihood, you will be perceived as a carrier of the bubonic plague and will be treated like Typhoid Mary. (In some instances, the older employees close to retirement will offer the most resistance to change or will look toward solidifying their position in order to ride out their last few years with the company.)

This PYA doctrine does not only apply to people to whom you are directly selling. It carries forward to everybody whom you meet in business, in any field. For example, someone you encounter at a conference, who is in an unrelated field but whose services would also appeal to your client base, will certainly cuddle up to you for leads, cross-selling, or joint projects. You should unabashedly do likewise.

So you see, everybody plays at flexible business ethics consciously or subconsciously. You need to play better and smarter, and maybe a touch more ruthless.

Business ethics, or the perception thereof, provoke timidity and intimidation in the weak entrepreneur, but for the one who understands the nature of the game and how to hone their skills to accommodate others' self-interests while getting what they want, the opportunities are limitless.

Social Norms May Not Apply to You. That's Okay Too.

- Question everything.
- Don't be governed by the ordinary.
- Be fair and respectful only if it works to your advantage.
- Do not accept other people's limitations that they place on themselves, or on you.
- Define success … just for you, what it means for you.
- Listen, watch, listen some more, and identify the weaknesses in your opponent.

In business, particularly in any networking situation or where you find yourself "on stage," such as selling a product/service, or promoting yourself at a trade show or conference, you may need to take on the role of the businessperson you want others to see. This is another prime example of "playacting," similar to theater. Assume the role and stay in character, particularly if the character is one you may not be 100 percent comfortable with. Your anxiety will be reduced by role-playing (covered in great detail later).

This Is How It Works in Real Life

For as long as I can remember, I hated trade shows and conferences. While I understood their value for connecting, networking, and pitching,

I always felt that the event was too superficial for lasting relationship building. The pace was too fast, and everyone had their own evident needs, like business speed dating.

What I always did was contact the event organizer in advance and request an attendees list, citing that I was unable to make it because of some out-of-town commitment, or a similar story. The lists usually contained contact information, names, and websites.

With the list in hand, I would screen the attendees for people/companies worth approaching. I would then call each up and say, "You may not remember me, but we met at the XXX show. Yes, it was so busy and you were swamped. I really liked your booth and your company info. Let's meet for a coffee (or lunch) and we can talk in a calmer setting than the show." As a matter of fact, many of them would actually say they remembered meeting me! In 99 percent of the time, it worked. There you go. Flexible ethics in action.

CHAPTER 7

Use the System.
Rule the System.

Know the rules well, so you can break them effectively.
Dalai Lama XIV

A "System" implies a coordinated, organized, well-defined arrangement, whereby the parties cooperate in a symbiotic relationship to achieve results. The "Business System," however, is more like an ambitious free-for-all.

In the "Business System," companies have a singular responsibility: contributing to their bottom line and thereby rewarding the shareholders. It is a game. Some players are voracious antagonists. Others are docile spectators. In between are the more gifted competitors who learn how the system works, what others expect of them, and how to manipulate others to gain advantage. That should be you.

Shifting Norms, Morals, and Scruples

Have the standards of what is acceptable conduct changed? Possibly, but even the bygone days have exhibited their share of dubious business behavior. What has changed is that (a) every sector of business has become a globally competitive environment; (b) technology has hastened the process of change; and (c) communication, including social media, has created "in-your-face" information dissemination. Nothing is sacred. Sound bites sell advertising and everything, even the trivial, seems to be considered newsworthy.

So while it may appear that our business scruples have become emancipated, that is not necessarily the case. Business has always been, and continues to be, a brutal world. It's just that the world has become smaller, more competitive, and more transparent, and you need to play the game shrewder and be more streetwise. Using the system is artful. Be wily.

Let's be clear: Using the system implies being clever in how you conduct yourself. It is the employment of strategies whereby you and your business are the primary beneficiaries. It insinuates actions you undertake that others may not engage in, or even think of, but which give you, the successful entrepreneur, resources with which to be more competitive in today's cutthroat business climate.

Using People as Stepping Stones

People in business are there to be used, meaning use people to get to other people. There are three distinct groups.

1. Those who direct you to prospective clients.
2. "Multipliers" who can refer you to businesspeople who can refer you to people who might steer you toward direct clients.
3. "Useless people" who cannot deliver on 1 and 2, and should be quickly screened for their lack of usability. If nothing is apparent, then ditch them fast.

Focus on the multipliers who have proven themselves to you, as they can open a multitude of direct leads. Use them wisely and often.

Getting Used Lets You Use Others Too

Exchanging favors and opportunities is a two-way street. Expect others to seek leads, contacts, and introductions from you. In fact, offer even before being asked, as that builds trust and openness and, more importantly, allows you to do likewise. And when such an opportunity presents itself to you, don't be shy.

After all, you have paid the admission price for the interaction, and delivered information or contacts that are valuable to the other party but of little use to you.

Only dead fish go with the flow.

Andy Hunt

The "System" Awaits You

- Keep your game plan somewhat flexible because situations change as you get farther along in your business.
- Don't treat any two clients the same. You may be overlooking certain subtleties that can cost you business.
- Never underestimate your clients. Their facade may be to play dumb (the old country-bumpkin routine). Even if they really are dumb, don't take the chance.
- Never take the opening lead in any new relationship, be it with client or contact. You need the time to size them up before you commit yourself. Their approach will dictate your reciprocal play.
- Look and listen. It sounds easy, but it's not. Your impulse, at a first encounter, will be to launch into your pitch. Hold back and keep the conversation going while you read the individual and their needs.
- Study psychology and behavioral patterns. They are as important as business journals. Learn to recognize patterns.
- Settle for excellence. That way, nobody can fault you.
- Learn patience. If someone is not calling you back, it doesn't mean they are not interested. They may just be too busy, or simply playing you.
- Price wars are self-defeating.
- Don't be impressed or overwhelmed by the facade of business—the gaudy reception area or the flamboyant conference room. These mean nothing, except that they can afford to pay the fair market price for your wares.
- Remember, you are dealing with an individual and, no matter how high up the management ladder your potential client has ascended, they look like anyone else with their clothes off.
- Be proud of your accomplishments, but remember not to brag so much that you will be perceived as pompous or obnoxious. Keep in mind that if your successes far exceed those of the person you are talking to, jealousy may come into play, and the relationship becomes lopsided and unworkable.

- You cannot ever win a fight with a client. The business community is smaller than you might imagine, and any short-term victories will cost you in credibility and reputation. Be a gracious survivor.
- "How are you?" is a salutation, not an invitation to list off your problems and maladies. Some people I have encountered have built their whole approach on making others feel sorry for them. They really tick me off. Besides which, I can easily match them ache for ache, problem for problem.
- Learn the art of compromise (flexible ethics) because anybody who goes into any situation with a fixed set of rules and expectations is asking for frustration and disaster.
- Exploit any and all support systems. This includes media and social media and bloggers' hype in the form of stories and articles about your company or accomplishments. Journalists hate to write, so if you do it for them and they can sell it or pawn it off as theirs, you can get loads of free publicity. Even trade associations, whose primary goal is to collect fees and build a mystique around their particular sector, are excellent candidates for intros and leads among their membership. Businessmen like joining associations. It may actually do some good, and sounds impressive. And if you want to be nominated for Businessperson of the Year, whether you merit it or not, just cozy up to the association director. It's great PR.
- Avoid vulnerability, be it financial shortfalls or any other facet of your business that leaves your flank exposed. Just because you know better than to go after your competition, it doesn't mean that they are similarly astute.
- The Peter Principle is alive and well and residing at most large companies: "People in a hierarchy tend to rise to their level of incompetence" (Peter 1969). Not to belittle the excellent, gifted executives that I have met over the course of my career, but the amount of deadwood is mind-boggling. Some organizations exist because of their well-entrenched market and profit margins established over years of enterprise. They are riding on their laurels from a long time ago and haven't been hit by any rude awakening ... yet. Again, the importance of sizing up the individual cannot be overemphasized. The vice president of finance may be brilliant or may be a

zombie. Don't go by the title. You are dealing with an individual (remember hearing that before?).

- Don't get caught up in the claptrap facade of business lingo. "Good corporate citizen," "environmentally friendly," and "commitment to product" are but a few catchphrases in the marketing world's image building. Don't believe the hype. It's for tourists.

Use the system, but don't let it swallow you.

This Is How It Works in Real Life

Downtime or vacation time for an entrepreneur is a challenge. Customers are always tugging at your sleeve, and your availability is an asset they count on.

When I needed to get away, I would work feverishly to complete my contracts to a presentable point, for example, a draft report, proposal, or study. I would then visit the client and say "Here is a draft. There's a lot in here. I really need you to spend a couple of weeks going through it, making notations, and discussing it with your people. Prepare any questions or comments to discuss. I will reconnect with you in 2 weeks to go over it all." Then I would disappear. It worked every time. It was a godsend strategy. Just ask my wife and kids!

CHAPTER 8

The Human Instinct to Fight on Another Day

Always remember that the crowd that applauds your coronation is the same crowd that will applaud your beheading. People like a show.

Terry Pratchett

Business Survival Instincts

We are all hardwired to survive. It's a human imperative and is our most powerful drive. Our "fight-or-flight" instinct assures that we give ourselves the best chance to live to fight another day. That is, the strongest and best equipped survive and the weakest hopefully enjoy their short time on this earth.

Darwin's Theory of Natural Selection is clearly evident in business. Those that exhibit strong survival skills manage to evolve and dominate and blossom. The rest, the hangers-on, the also-rans, the ambivalent, the fixated, the lazy, the insecure, well, they generally evaporate.

Winners have a strong fight-or-flight reflex. They sense opportunity and pounce. They sense danger and retreat to safety, always ready to re-emerge with a new plan. Winners have a gut feel that acts as a safety net, and they listen to that "go/no-go" voice in their heads.

Your gut feel is your safety valve. One of the biggest mistakes entrepreneurs make is disregarding their instincts. Don't ever let greed dictate your decision making, and, at the other extreme, obey any sense of danger, red flags, or impending doom. And remember, most missteps are not fatal, more like hiccups. Get past them. And try not to listen to others' horror stories about business. They are theirs alone.

Business Pain Relief. A Checkup to Measure Your Pain.

Complete an assessment on the health and direction of your business and how well you personally deal with the challenges (and opportunities) as an entrepreneur. This is especially critical if you are having issues with your business or you are seeking future-forward direction. Think of this as a proprietary "Business Pain Relief" checkup.

Each line contains a question for you to consider and then rate your response to it.

Fill in the following chart by ticking one of the column boxes, which range from 1 (low) to 5 (high). What do they mean? Example: Are you hardworking? If hard work is very important to you, then tick column 5 adjacent to the question. If not, then choose the degree of lesser importance (1–4).

- 1 = no, absolute zero priority to me, or does not apply to me
- 2 = no, not very important to me
- 3 = maybe, sometimes, rarely
- 4 = yes, important to me
- 5 = yes, absolutely highest priority

Once you complete these as honestly as possible, have this Business Checkup reviewed by a trusted associate, that is, someone who has been there and is there every single day. Someone who signs paychecks for others.

Wherever you see a successful business, someone made a courageous decision.

Peter F. Drucker

Let's get started. There are four categories for you to review. Each deals with a separate part of your business.

1. **Marketing Business Health Checkup** deals with all aspects of your marketing, branding, competition, marketing avenues (including online and social media), and communication strategy.
2. **Finance Business Health Checkup** focuses on your financial health, collecting invoices, paying bills, cash flow, costs and margins, and your ability for cash flow management.
3. **Corporate Business Health Checkup** questions your corporate policy, vision, employees, business planning, and effective human resources.
4. **Business Start-up/Expansion Health Checkup** is solely for new business ventures or for those looking to expand and diversify their business into new areas and territories.

MARKET/MARKETING Business Health Checkup: Ask Yourself	1	2	3	4	5
Do you have a clear understanding of your target market?					
Are you effectively reaching your customers?					
Are you clear who your competitors are?					
Are you different from your competitors?					
Have you surveyed your customers to get feedback?					
If yes, have you adopted your customers' recommendations?					
Do you know why people buy from you?					
Have you actively measured the quality of what you produce/sell/provide before a complaint is received?					
Have you developed a profile of who your customers are?					
Do you know the age, income, marital status of your customers?					
Do you know your customers' buying habits?					
Do you need to educate your customers or build awareness of what you do?					
Do you have a marketing and communication plan?					
If yes, are you following it? Tracking it?					
Do you have an identifiable brand?					
Is your website effective? Do you know?					
Is your advertising effective? Do you know?					
Is your online/social media presence effective? Do you know?					

MARKET/MARKETING Business Health Checkup: Ask Yourself	1	2	3	4	5
Do you understand the trends in your business sector?					
Do you know your market share?					
Do you monitor competition pricing?					
Do you have others selling your products/services? Are they effective?					
Do you use professional marketing consultants?					
Do you monitor the activity on your website?					
Do you update your website regularly?					
Do you track which products/services sell the most, and why?					
Do you reward your existing customers?					

FINANCE Business Health Checkup: Ask Yourself	1	2	3	4	5
Do you analyze your supplier invoices and terms for accuracy?					
Do you run monthly performance versus budget financials?					
Do you generate cash flow projections?					
Are you meeting financial commitments to suppliers and government?					
Is your cash flow strong, and can it support the daily operation of the business?					
Are your customers meeting your payment terms?					
Do you generate and review monthly management reports?					
Can you identify risks that may dramatically impact the future of your business?					
Do you monitor your gross margins and adjust for changes?					
Do you monitor your inventory to determine turnovers/year?					
Do you have a good working relationship with your bank?					
Are your prices competitive?					
Are your profits in line with industry standards?					
Do you anticipate immediate or short-range gains or results?					
Are your revenues meeting projected sales?					

Corporate Business Health Checkup: Ask Yourself	1	2	3	4	5
Are your staff fulfilling their responsibilities?					
Are you in control of the day-to-day activities your business undertakes—tasks planned, scheduled, and prioritized?					
Is the culture in your business positive?					
Do you run security checks on your data?					
Is your intellectual property secure?					
Are you open to your team's input and suggestions?					
Do you have regular staff meetings for reviews, brainstorming ideas?					
Do you have a Business Plan?					
Are you meeting your Business Plan milestones and target levels?					
Do you offer your people bonuses or performance incentives?					
Do you have up-to-date Job Descriptions for employee positions?					
Have you designed an Exit Strategy for yourself?					
BUSINESS START-UP/EXPANSION Health Checkup: Ask Yourself	**1**	**2**	**3**	**4**	**5**
Have you set up an Advisory Board to use as a sounding board?					
Have you pinpointed the exact markets your idea is expected to tap into?					
Is your idea an original, new concept, or is it a new combination or adaptation?					
Are the projected returns adequate?					
Are the risk factors acceptable?					
Have you checked the idea for faults or limitations?					
How simple or complex will the idea's execution or implementation be?					
Does your idea have a natural sales appeal?					
Is the market ready for it?					
Do you know that customers can afford it?					
Can your company be competitive?					
Does your idea fill an identified need?					
Have you done research on your competition?					

BUSINESS START-UP/EXPANSION Health Checkup: Ask Yourself	1	2	3	4	5
Have you considered the possibility of user resistance or difficulties?					
Have you had others review your idea?					
Have you generated a Business Plan with financial and cash projections?					
Have you examined all the costs involved?					
Have you identified the level of risk?					
Have you identified all launch costs?					
Do you know for sure your customers want what you will be offering?					

Four Basic Survival Fundamentals

1. Know your audience. Try to learn exactly what makes them tick, either from information gleaned from associates or the industry in general or by remaining alert and being extremely observant and perspicacious at all encounters. Don't let your guard down. Instead, listen to what is being said and how the conversation flows and observe the body language, temperament, and interest level. This all-important skill will be discussed in detail later on.

2. Recognize the need of the client or contact, and mold your approach and product offerings to fulfill their very specific interests. Are their needs oriented toward personal development, corporate, networking, and/or career path? Find out. Everyone, including the entrepreneur, is in a virtual state of flux and jockeying toward certain goals. Help them meet those targets and you will succeed.

3. Take advantage of situations that can better yourself and advance your own cause. Don't be shy to court people who can furnish you with leads and reciprocate in kind.

4. Do what you have to do, and in any way you can, in order to succeed. Although the boundaries are flexible, they certainly preclude dishonesty, which is just plain wrong. Otherwise, almost everything else is fair game. Let your conscience govern your restraint. I knew a heavy-equipment agricultural leasing agent who, armed with an

investment calculator, worked out the leasing rates for his prospective clients. Regardless of the cost of the equipment or the worth of the customer, the lease rates always came out to 14.1 percent. It was preprogrammed. Is that flexible ethics?

Business is easy. It's so easy to make things complicated in business.

David Green

Avoid Nasty E-mails and Burning Bridges

While it may be satisfying to launch into noxious e-mails (or social media posts), or burning bridges to exact revenge, or out of frustration, don't do it. Rebuilding relationships is tenuous at best, and, once rebuilt, rarely displays the same degree of trust as before the dustup.

A business truism: Whomever you alienate will find an occasion to return the favor downstream, either directly or by trashing you to others. You have a tiff with "A" who dismembers you to "B" and you lose an order from "B" and you never know why. It can get very personal, and it is as certain as the law of gravity. It's also just dumb business.

Relationships take time to build and effort to maintain. Even where the other party is a reprehensible troll, if they can be of any use to you, clench your buttocks and smile.

Don't Buy Toys

There are more action items to consider and adopt aside from not writing toxic e-mails or posts, and not alienating people who might serve a purpose other than target practice. Here they are:

- Use your capital and cash flow to build your business and not your ego.
- When business is slow or your market recedes, businesspeople tend to cut marketing costs. Wrong! Increase your marketing budget instead. Marketing drives sales, which drives cash flow.
- Diversify your risk. Do not put all your faith in one service or product line. Get beyond that dangerous complacency.

- Monitor your revenue, by product, and cut your unprofitable and unproductive items.
- Clear obsolete and slow inventory. Don't hoard.
- Create backup plans for any identifiable contingencies. Things change, so prepare to change too.
- Do regular market, industry, and competition research. You don't want surprises. Ever.
- Be decisive. Don't procrastinate. Make a decision and act on it.
- Be proactive. Business does not walk through your doors.
- Consider growth by acquisition as a way to grow. It represents exponential growth and, interestingly enough, helps streamline competition too.
- Repeat customers and clients can represent more than 80 percent of your revenues. So before you spend all your time chasing new business, focus on coddling your existing clients, and show real appreciation with great customer service, rewards, perks, and recognition. The restaurant maître d' who remembers your name is showing customer appreciation ... and you love it, don't you?
- Listen to what your clients are saying. They may just be right. They can also become your un-clients very quickly if you don't listen and react.
- Remain mentally strong and enthusiastic, even if you have to fake it.
- Hire people to do stuff you don't like, or are not skilled to do.
- Spend your time doing what you do best. For example, if you need techie stuff like websites, a social media presence, blasts, or blogs, then hire a geek.
- Cash really is king (or queen). It also buys you time to get over any down cycles.
- Don't trash competition much. You cannot build a business on someone else's back.
- Stay viable. You cannot succeed if you do not survive.

This Is How It Works in Real Life

One of the businesses I owned was a joint venture in Russia, with an office in St. Petersburg. The company was engaged in button cell and lithium battery production as well as titanium medical equipment cases and bicycle parts. The plant itself was huge, but my office only had a staff of four, including a driver/bodyguard who chauffeured me around during my visits and attended all my meetings. Don't ask.

Once our contracts were done, I decided that, with the surge in Russian mafioso and their chubby little fingers in every pie, it was wise to walk away (while I could still walk).

My staff and overheads were not huge, but these four people and their families depended on me. I could not simply, in good conscience, walk away.

I gathered them together, explained the situation, told them the business was done, but gave them 6 months to find another job. The office remained open so they could use the computers and supplies. I gave them glowing letters of reference and helped them draft English language resumes to present to the hordes of new western and European multinationals now entering the "free enterprise" (?) Russian economy.

They kept asking "What do we do when we come in every day here?" My answer was "Find a job. That's it. Just find something. You have 6 months. And meanwhile, you will keep getting a salary while you look for something good. You all have families and kids. I have met them all. They are good people. Just find a job."

They all did, in less than 6 months. And I stayed in touch, and even did business with some of them for years. What was the cost of doing the right thing? Immeasurable.

Everyone needs to survive.

CHAPTER 9

The Psychology of Business

Sometimes being the only one that isn't desperate to be noticed is what makes them pay attention.

Morley, LA Street Artist

Psychology, as it applies to business, identifies how and why people make decisions. Applied psychology helps you quantify the hierarchy of relationships; determine the most effective strategies in marketing, selling, and dealmaking; and identify how to effectively communicate with your team, your clients, and your network connections. It allows you to motivate others and maneuver people to act in your best interest.

Understand and appeal directly to what the potential customer is getting out of dealing with you, and what triggers them to respond positively to you. If, for example, you are selling a service that makes that person's job easier, gives them more free time, or more time to do what they enjoy or do best, or makes them look good to their superiors, they will more than likely deal with you. Those motivators are called the "hot buttons." Good entrepreneurs identify and use them effectively.

A Behavioral Psychology Quickie

Here are two examples whereby psychology very subtly plays such an important part of everyday decision making. The ramifications to business are pretty compelling.

Question: Two cookie jars. One is full. The other jar has only three cookies left. The subjects are offered a cookie from either jar. Which do people choose?

Answer: The one with three cookies. It is perceived as having something special that others are reaching for. How does that apply to your marketing? Are you offering anything special? Different? Is it a question of supply and demand?

Question: Why do waiters who bring customers candies with their bill get 23 percent higher tips? Answer: Because in the customer's mind, they show they are caring, even if they really don't. How's your customer service?

You Really, Truly Need to Know What Motivates Others

A concern about appearing honest may outweigh our desire to actually be honest even in situations where it will cost us money to lie.
Shoham Choshen-Hillel, "General Lying to Appear Honest,"
Journal of Experimental Psychology, January 30, 2020

It is important to recognize the patterns of motivation in order to fully comprehend how to manipulate the people you will be dealing with in the business world.

Understand these and you will master how to control people in every conceivable business situation. Once you tune in to what they want and need from you, then play into them.

These are the "hot buttons," that is, what motivates people to act, in order of priority within each category. Use these motivators to your full advantage. They are your source of power and advantage. (Note: Some items appear on more than one list, but in a different hierarchy of importance.)

Ambition
- climbing the social ladder
- wealth, greed
- promotions
- power
- recognition by peers
- career path (long-term planning)
- building a following

- status
- contacts and connections
- favors (IOU's for cashing in later)
- survival
- greed (ambition gone berserk)

PYA (Protect Your ***)
- caution
- fear of doing anything wrong that can be blamed on them
- longevity
- acceptance by peers
- recognition by management
- stability (status quo)
- promotion
- wealth

Status Quo
- ego, pride
- fear of change
- timidity, that is, lack of conviction

Unpredictable
- revenge against company or "the system"
- apathy
- incompetence

Aside from "unpredictable," all the others are clearly identifiable motives which you absolutely must learn to recognize in people and situations, in order to fully capitalize on every opportunity and in each and every encounter. You must also learn to "play" on people's needs and motives. Role-play to fine-tune those skills. Everybody does something for a reason. Nothing is by accident.

Don't believe everything you don't hear.

Dan Waldschmidt

The Three Most Influential Motivational "Hot Buttons"

- **Ego**—people like to be made to feel important, or special. It is human nature. When you buy a pair of Nike sneakers and you see the bold check mark on the side of the shoe, that is appealing to your ego. It is telling you that you are great and you are strong. Is it unethical to appeal to people's ego?
- **Flattery/Pride**—how often have you walked into a clothing store, tried something on, and been told that it makes you look younger or slimmer? Does the store owner mean it, or are they bending the ethical rules slightly and harmlessly to get the sale?
- **Greed**—everyone likes to feel that they are getting a deal. That is why stores have markdowns, sales, suggested list prices slashed, Boxing Day sales, two-for-one sales, and more. Are the sellers losing money? Lost leaders bring in more traffic.

The Psychology of Influencing People: Play the Head Games Effectively

Get people to buy, change attitudes, build excitement, enhance your image, build loyalty, and extract referrals—these are all doable by applying the principles of psychology into business.

- **Reciprocity**: the equitable exchange of valued assets, namely ideas, contacts, favors, and leads.
- **Commitment and Consistency**: Try to assure that the prospective client agrees with what you are proposing. That early commitment has a greater chance of leading to a contract or sale. Newsletter sign-ups are one type of extracting an early commitment.
- **Social Proof:** Work to establish a comfort level for the customer. Where somebody else likes the product, as expressed in a testimonial or commercial, that is validation. For example, in the travel and accommodation industry, the host will often ask you to post a positive comment on Trip Advisor, Travelocity or Lonely Planet.
- **Liking**: Whoever represents the company needs to be likeable. This improves the chances of doing business.

- **Authority**: People respond to authority and celebrities. Companies use "pitchmen" who are well recognized, such as sports figures or recognized actors (or pretend doctors) to influence decision makers.
- **Scarcity:** Based on "supply and demand," limited-time offers and limited availability are two techniques promoting scarcity.

Influencing people is also the cornerstone of every business book on marketing and selling. "The influence of yes" highlights how the behavioral building blocks of psychology can be applied in the business world. These are powerful tools for you to apply in all your business dealings.

Human Need: Another Psychological Business Trigger

Human need governs decision making. Everybody has needs, but, if you can catalog, in broad strokes, what those needs are, and build them into your products or business behavior, you can then influence people to act to your advantage by triggering any of the following:

- Avoidance of pain
- Comfort, both physical and emotional
- Gaining pleasure
- Need for new stimuli
- Feeling of closeness
- Ability to be involved
- Personalization

Just as important is our "perception of need." That is, creating need in the minds of the client.

One such additional psychological influencer is novelty. People have a curiosity about the unknown. Novelty, it is said, activates the brain. Apple is the master of novelty, introducing new innovative products that we didn't even know we needed.

Finally, using business psychology in everyday situations such as team building, leadership, and human resources can also be explored at https://www.fundera.com/blog/psychology-101-can-help-run-better-business (Meredith Wood, Fundera).

The Fine Art of Gentle and Subtle Persuasion

If and when you tell people what to do, they can often become defensive. That's human nature. We are territorial beasts. But, if you lead them to arrive at the same conclusion as yours all by themselves, they are far more likely to buy what you're selling. The key action here is "lead."

Think of it like a parent–child relationship where you don't command your youngster to eat the oatmeal. Instead you make it fun, show them you are eating it too, make a game of it, and watch them dig in. You lead. Think of it that way and you can't lose.

There are a few tricks to changing somebody's mind without force-feeding them.

- Ask questions that lead the other party toward the decision that you want. Stop selling. Start directing.
- Give people options to choose from. And while you focus moreso on the option you want them to choose by also giving the person alternatives, that makes it seem like the decision is theirs alone.
- The person you are dealing with will have a need, that is, what they want or desire to achieve, and where they are at now, that likely being at a shortfall to filling their need. That is the "gap," and that is your primary target.
- Be empathetic and understanding, and listen. Just be quiet and hear what is being said, or asked of you, and respond in a thoughtful manner. In the end, you will get what you want, and so will the other party.

Why People Deal with You

Why do people deal with you? They are not necessarily being "nice." That's a false comfort. They are being selfish. What you do for them is their primary motivation. Never lose sight of that. They may "like" you, but it's your usefulness to them that they like even more.

Why Winners Win

Winners win because they want to. They are driven to and are oblivious to any distractions or weaknesses. They are always "on." They impress the heck out of everyone, and often themselves as well. Winners win because they make things happen regardless of what others may say. At the risk of sounding like a sports product cliche, they "just do it".

Why Losers Lose

Losers visualize the penalties of failure and associate failure with pain. Winners visualize the rewards of success. Your attitude and outlook dictate everything.

Maslow's "Hierarchy of Needs" Applied to Business

Abraham Maslow[1] developed a motivational pyramid model of human needs, from the most basic needs like food, shelter, and safety at the bottom of the pyramid to the highest, most elite needs including emotional satisfaction. It is a stepped process, whereby each lower tier need must be achieved before the person can advance to the next highest step. This process is called "self-actualization." Here is the **Hierarchy of Needs** adapted to a business perspective.

1. **Physiological** needs (the lowest achievable need on the pyramid) demand the person to seek water, sleep, and food. Business parallels encompass meeting physiological needs with items such as training materials, accounting software or business planning tools.
2. Next on the pyramid is **Safety**, generally described as security, shelter, and protection. The business analogy includes insurance, alarm systems, retirement security, and investments.
3. **Belongingness** is the third tier and includes basic emotional needs such as love, friendship, and acceptance by others. Its business partners might well be clothing, grooming products, entertainment, clubs and resorts, bars, and even dating sites and services.
4. Reaching toward the top, we find **Ego** as the next need. This need caters to prestige, status, and accomplishment. Appropriate business

---

[1]Cherry, K. March 16, 2020. "Biography of Abraham Maslow (1908–1970)." *History and Biographies*. https://www.verywellmind.com/biography-of-abraham-maslow-1908-1970-2795524, (date accessed June 10, 2020).

offerings include money, luxury cars, credit cards, houses/condos, country club memberships, and other status possessions. This need is targeted by a plethora of products and services, particularly in our western greedy and relentless need for social prominence. Do you want a Honda Fit or an Acura? Hmm, tough choice.

5. Finally, sitting at the top of the pyramid is the much sought after **Self-actualization**, as depicted by self-fulfillment and enrichment (sigh, don't we all seek this level). This is fulfilled with travel, education, and spiritual experiences. The euphoria of success!

This begs the question that knowing where your product or service fits in, how you will fulfill those human needs, and is there an awareness in the market that you are playing in that tier? As well, understand that the higher your product or service caters within that pyramid, the smaller and more "elite" your market becomes.

Don't live the same year 75 times and call it a life.

Robin Sharma

"The Selfish (Business) Gene": We Are All Selfish

The Selfish Gene (Richard Dawkins, 1976) builds on the principal theory expounded by George C. Williams's *Adaptation and Natural Selection* (1966). While it discusses the predominance of dominating genes in our DNA makeup, it has morphed into "the survival of the fittest" among us. It is competition focused, even "dog-eat-dog," which is a further bastardization of The Selfish Gene theory. The essence, then, can be distilled into a key principle of behavior that can be directly applied to business.

People act of their own self-interest. Everything we do is inherently selfish. When we give to a charity, we do it because it makes us feel good about ourselves. When someone purchases a product or contracts your service, they do it to satisfy their personal interests. Make sure you flatter people and tell them how wonderful, smart, and successful you think they are (whether you mean it or not), and, coincidentally, that they will become increasingly moreso when they deal with you.

From an entrepreneurial perspective, that "selfish gene" needs to also be in your DNA makeup. That means doing for you, not just for others.

Become "business-selfish" to cope, survive, grow, and succeed. Let others worry about themselves. You take care of you.

When you go into business for yourself, you do it for you, first and foremost, and that is fine too. If others around you benefit from your efforts, that's a rewarding secondary effect. Don't go into business just for everybody else except yourself. Martyrdom is not fashionable in the business milieu.

Greed and Revenge

Greed and revenge are two of the most destructive reasons to do anything in business. Yet, time and again, I have seen these cited by clients as a motive in price undercutting, negative advertising and, even worse, inflating a contract/sale with no consideration to repeat business. Each contract/sale should not be your last one with a client, but instead, the first of many. Worship your existing and critically important repeat clients.

And Pavlov Had His Dogs

Pavlovian conditioning demonstrated the ability to trigger dogs to salivate when they learned to recognize a repeatable stimulus, such as the sound of a bell. It became a behavioral reflex.

So how do we humans react when we are continuously bombarded by "in-your-face" product logos or the image of a well-recognized actor hawking whatever? We salivate. Anybody else hear that bell?

Even Socrates Understood Selfishness

In Plato's *Republic*, Socrates's older brother, Glaucon, acknowledges that people's behavior is rooted in their own self-interest. "Even the most 'just' man would act purely for themselves and not care if they harmed anyone in the process."[2] Further, Glaucon went on to theorize that people only do the right thing because they fear being punished if they get caught.

---

[2]Pappas, S. March 27, 2017. "Are Humans Inherently Selfish?" *Wellness* https://www.huffpost.com/entry/are-humans-inherently-selfish_n_58b4544ee4b0780bac2bccf0, (date accessed June 10, 2020).

Selfishness is age-old and a psychological principle, whereby you appeal to the selfish nature of your audience. It is a readily applied business tactic.

Psychological Egoism and Hedonism: More Selfish Behavior

Now we are into the somewhat outlandish, but still useful motivational drivers that entrepreneurs should be aware of.

Psychological Egoism dictates that people are motivated not only by their own self-interest, but also by helping others fulfill their self-interest because it makes them look good or feel good, or, more importantly, be perceived favorably by others. So much for the purity of altruism!

Psychological Hedonism states that "the ultimate motive for voluntary action is the desire to experience pleasure or to avoid pain ... Immediate gratification can be sacrificed for a chance of greater, future pleasure."[3]

What Does All This Mean?

In reviewing this particular chapter, I would be somewhat remiss in not apologizing to the reader. You have been bombarded with every conceivable motivator and driver that can direct business to your company. You have been exposed to the doctrine of self-interest, greed, pride, ego, hedonism, egoism, and every other "-ism" in the book of pushing people's hot buttons to act.

In doing so, there was a concerted effort to present everything so that you could find something, some psychological thread, that you can comfortably build into your company, your offerings, and even your business persona. You now have a great deal of food for thought and tons of mind games and psychobabble to choose from.

The takeaway here is that selfishness rules supreme, be it physical or emotional, and that at the end of the day, people are people. Knowing

---

[3]Wikipedia. "Psychological Egoism." https://en.wikipedia.org/wiki/Psychological_egoism, (date accessed June 10, 2020).

how and why they act greatly enhances your chances to score on everything from controlling people and dealmaking to closing sales. It's all a matter of exploiting the rules of human nature and becoming somewhat of an empath to tune in to people and deliver what they need.

This Is How It Works in Real Life

I had a client in the chemical business. Pretty dull, but highly profitable. His plant was old and located in an area that was undergoing urban sprawl. He discussed with me the opportunity to move to a newer location. He wanted me to do a business case study.

I asked him why, since he was not being forced to move. I told him he was crazy, and then started questioning him about the "real" reasons behind the relocation. I knew my client well and sensed there were other circumstances at play.

Apparently, 40 years earlier, his uncle, ready to retire, had handed the business over to him for $1. Now that uncle's son was employed at the company, and my client, reaching retirement age, wanted to do the same for his nephew with a clean succession.

We worked out a plan for succession with the continuity of remaining in the existing facility, thereby avoiding moving costs, which would have included prohibitive regulatory/environmental issues due to the nature of the business. Everyone was pleased.

I may have lost a contract for a business case study, but by knowing my client, listening, and understanding his decision making "hot buttons," I became his trusted business adviser forever.

CHAPTER 10

"What's in It for Me"(WIIFM) Thinking

No matter what story you tell, make the buyer the hero.

Chris Brogan

There are two connotations of 'What's in it for Me' (WIIFM) thinking, namely (1) how it applies directly to you personally and (2) how WIIFM applies to others with whom you are dealing.

WIIFM for You, and Only You. Consider Yourself Number 1

You have a responsibility to yourself. That implies your physical (health), financial (wealth), emotional (stress), and core relationship (family) well-being. The nuance here relates to how you plan your business, whether it be start-up, acquisition, merger, strategic partnership, divestiture, expansion or full-blown growth. In these instances, you need to be astonishingly selfish. You and you alone are number 1.

Consideration needs to be given to the impact of any decision on you, the prima donna in the room, the focus of your own personal attention. Do only what's good for you, not just what might be expected from you. Every decision, every idea, and everything you do needs to be beneficial to number 1—you, and only you.

Sometimes business requires you to be ruthless, obsessive, and callous, but always remember, you are the only person you need to look out for. Everyone else is just there to fulfill that personal goal. However, there is a major proviso here, there needs to be an important balancing act in you also assuring that your customers WIIFM needs are met. This high wire balancing act can be precarious, but so very necessary.

WIIFM for Customers: Translate Facts into Benefits

WIIFM thinking is what *every* customer will ask. So, be prepared. Know your targets and cater to them. WIIFM should be in every contact, communication, and pitch. After all, it's not what you want to sell or promote, it's what the target wants and needs that's important.

Keep the WIIFM thinking in mind, and zero in not on what you can deliver, but instead what you can provide that will meet the customers' needs.

So, exactly what can you actually deliver to a client? Service, price, quality, blah, blah. Yes, everybody pitches those. Here are what else clients react to:

- You make it easier for them to do their job or run their own business.
- You make them look good (and more likely to get promotions, bonuses, etc.)
- You do part of their job for them.
- You save them money.
- You increase their bottom line.
- You reduce their stress levels.
- You take a load off their workload.
- You free up time for them that they could be doing things they like or do better.
- You give them a sense of freedom.
- You give them peace of mind.
- You make them comfortable dealing with someone they can trust and rely on.

It's not how great your product or service is. That's your perspective, your marketing and sales pitch. Those are the facts. It's what it can do for others. Those are the benefits.

There is only one boss: the customer. And he can fire everybody in the company simply by spending his money somewhere else.

Sam Walton

Figure out what they need and expect by probing conversation. Be a good listener. Then tell them what they need to hear. "This will attract more traffic to your website. Past clients report an uptick of 21 percent." "Our products will reduce your costs by 16 percent and even decrease your wastage." "Our security systems give you real-time protection that has proven to reduce inventory shrinkage between 6 percent and 8 percent. What's that worth to you in dollars?"

Don't sell them yet. First you need to get them interested before you pitch how wonderful you and your company are. If you launch as a pitchman too early, you will lose their attention. They may "like" what you are selling, but they will only buy if it delivers something for them. The trick is to identify what that "something" is.

You need to see that glint of recognition in the other person's eyes. That sparkle confirms you have found their hot button motivational trigger that tells you that they are now listening. Until that actually happens, you can assume that while you are talking, they are replaying the theme song from Bohemian Rhapsody in their head.

If that kind of "aha moment" coincides with the other party asking for more information about you, your company, or your offerings, then you can go into pitchman mode. But not until then.

If they look at their watch or phone while you are still talking, you might as well quit your spiel. You are done.

Let's Be Clear about WIIFM (and Don't Take This the Wrong Way)

This is my cup of care. Oh look, it's empty.

Zack O'Malley and Jordan Jenison

People don't really care about your product or service. Don't take it the wrong way, they may "like" what you are selling, but they will only "buy" if it delivers something for them.

Everybody has their own agenda, their own self-interest. It could be conscious, or even subconscious, but everyone shoulders their own baggage. You have something you want the audience to buy into. The audience has their own interests. Your one and only job is to align the two.

Far too often, businesspeople spend a great deal of time talking about themselves or their products/services, when they should be focusing almost entirely on their audience, and if what they are offering to sell or deliver actually hits the "hot buttons" of the person who needs to say "yes."

When you sell a hand cream, nobody really cares if it smells great or is made from the rare *Passiflora edulis* or passion fruit plant grown on the slopes of Paraguay. Big deal. No, they care that the cream will give them the complexion of a teenager, or a Victoria Secret runway model.

If you are marketing a website or graphics design service, nobody really cares that you have 20 years' experience and four college degrees. All they care about is that if you design and build a great website for them, it will make them look good and drive more traffic to their company site, which translates to more revenues and profit. So any sales pitch should emphasize the rewards to the customer.

It's not that people are uncaring. It's that people are driven by a "selfish gene," and if you want to succeed, you better learn to appeal to their self-interest. That is what gets them reaching for their credit card. That is WIIFM in action.

The "So What?" Effect

When you are selling or presenting, you need to visualize your audience saying "So what?" At a sales meeting with a client, put yourself in the recipient's place and be honest in asking yourself "So what? Why is that important to me? What will it do for me?" Follow that train of thought and assure that there is a special place for explaining just that in your communication.

This applies equally to any marketing materials, websites, social media campaigns, advertising, blogs, and marketing and promotion. Imagine the reader or viewer murmuring "So what?" Make sure anything you put forward demonstrates quantifiable deliverables for your audience. Facts, not hype. Facts.

WIIFM in Group Presentations

There is (yet) another acronym for building WIIFM into any presentation to a larger audience, say presenting an opportunity for investors, the buying group at BigDealStore, or an organization or body of government who have the ability to influence the issue you are there to present.

The acronym is ASIA (Audience, Solutions, Ideas, Action Plan). It refers to grabbing the attention of the audience right at the get-go by zeroing in on what is important to them.

It is logical. It presents the "hot buttons" in order to capture others' interest. It works.

1. **A = Audience**. Jump into the fray immediately, rather than a lengthy opening expounding on who you are, how great you are, how many titles in your credentials, and the beauty of your corporate logo. This is the issue, or opportunity. This is why we are here today. Here is the compelling data or valid justification to support today's center of attention for you, and for us. Get people involved immediately.

2. **S = Solution**. You now know the issue, or opportunity. Here are the solutions or actionable "moving forward" strategies to be proposed, with more details forthcoming in the presentation. Everyone is now on notice regarding all the parameters of the get-together. It is only at this point that you showboat ever so humbly who you are and that you are the right person for the challenge at hand.

3. **I = Ideas.** You have presented the framework and people are paying attention since you have also focused on their interests and WIIFM for themselves or their organization. It is now time to present how you intend to deliver. Even more important are those pesky facts, that is, what exactly you generate in deliverables. Remember, not just "deliver," but actual "deliverables/outcomes."

4. **A = Action Plan**. Milestones, timelines, quantifiable and trackable progress, step-by-step action items, allocation and division of responsibility and reporting. In short, how you specifically plan to work on your audience's behalf and meet their needs in doing so.

Your case is made and your essential ingredients have been laid before them. You have appealed to their WIIFM. They will be impressed. Well done.

A man's success in business today turns upon his power of getting people to believe he has something they want.

Gerald Stanley

WIIFM in Dealing with Employees and Managers

Interesting enough, the ASIA doctrine is very applicable to in-house team meetings. People detest change. They get nervous. They feel threatened. They wring their hands. They skip lunch to keep working. They delete all those game apps from their computers. They mentally prepare themselves for unwanted change, even where that change might be positive. Change is, after all, change.

By clearly presenting the issues for change (good or bad), the intended solutions, and the quantifiable impact on the human resources (staff, managers), the resistance to change is less impactful.

This Is How It Works in Real Life

Customer appreciation and loyalty is sometimes short-lived.

In one particular case, our firm had just succeeded in securing a major government grant package for our prized multinational account. When our next assignment came up and we went confidently to negotiate a contract with them, we were treated like poor relations from Transylvania.

When I questioned this attitude, and reminded them of what my company had delivered previously for them, I was told "Don't tell us what you've done for us in the past, but tell us what you can do for us now."

After carefully explaining what the expected deliverables were of our involvement (WIIFM), I did a classic "takeaway," my heart pounding as I packed my briefcase to leave. I wanted that new contract, but on my terms, not theirs. They were astounded, and said they now had a clearer understanding of our role, and that the expected benefits paralleled their needs. The contract was now ours.

Obviously I took the contract, but the confrontation took its toll on our relationship.

Use WIIFM in any and all sales presentations. At the same time, don't expect business from a client ad infinitum. You have to continually work for it.

CHAPTER 11

Planning Is Dreaming
and Scheming

What would you do if you weren't afraid?

Sheryl Sandberg

In planning, it is of paramount importance to not only understand the mechanics of what to do, but also to realize why you are doing it, what significance each move has, and the implications of your actions and inactions.

Setting Meaningful Goals beyond Your Reach

The true entrepreneur is a visionary who sets targets high, just beyond reach, and strives a little harder to stretch that extra distance. Goals, sometimes in conflict with each other, give you something to dream about.

Goals should be concrete as well as abstract. Material possessions or sales targets are concrete. Power and independence are decidedly abstract, but may be just as important to you.

A clear distinction must also be made between business and personal issues. The former can be deemed as a thriving enterprise, while the latter can mean money, friends, health, and/or family. See what I mean?

Goals can be conflicting. A concrete business goal might be to establish branch offices within 2 years. Simultaneously, a concrete personal goal can be to start taking long weekends and well-deserved vacations during that same time period. Something has to give, and the art of flexible ethics once again intercedes as a vital survival practice. In setting your goals, work toward compatibility with all your other priorities. Make them work together.

Please remember to do your goal setting with yourself in mind. You are the very reason you are in business. Reward yourself by setting personal aspirations that matter to you as goals.

You must learn to distinguish between a real objective versus "agenda-type" activity. "I want to own a Ferrari" (especially if you can't spell Lamborghini) is a real ambition. "I want to go to the car showroom" is an agenda-related activity since it is an action rather than an outcome.

Goals are traditionally well defined, but must also be totally flexible to change with circumstance. If things are going well, build your targets higher, and vice versa. If your personal life changes, such as marriage, children, or health issues, it is time to reassess your priorities and modify your goals accordingly.

And if this entire philosophical dissertation isn't confusing enough, another important variable in this entire scenario is "time." Try to be realistic in setting the time frame for achieving those goals, and depending on how your business and/or life is progressing, ongoing reappraisal may be in order as well.

Your Goals Are Your Mantra

Whatever your end goal in business might be, quantify it, print up a big poster in huge, colorful font, and put it over your workstation where you can be reminded of why you are doing this. Repeat it like a mantra when you've had a bad day, or when you're having a pity party. And as far as changing your goals, elevate them, but never downgrade to make them more easily achievable. That's just an excuse to fail.

Use "Baby Steps" in Planning

I believe that the process of getting into business, or growing an existing business, is a series of "Baby Steps."

If you were to list out all the stages you need to go through, set milestones and targets in terms of dates and achievable results, and prioritize these baby steps into a list of things to get done, you will have created an Action Plan.

A "Baby Step" is a simple, short-term achievable action that, when combined into a series of steps, gets you results. Anything in business, from start-ups to expanding your venture can be broken into baby steps. Want an analogy?

What steps do you go through getting out of bed? Well you shut the alarm, left leg out of bed followed by your right leg (or vice versa), scratch your respective body parts, put your slippers on, left then right, go to the bathroom, check your phone, etc.... see what I mean?

Baby steps in business are readily doable milestones. They motivate you. They inspire further progress. Keep moving forward at any pace, at any price. Avoid stagnation or complacency.

Hindsight in Planning: Keep Your Eyes Forward, Please

Hindsight is only good for occasionally learning from your successes (and failures). Otherwise, it is a waste of time and effort. The act of "living in the past" is destructive in business, especially when everything around you changes (consumer tastes, competition, technology, product/service leap-frogging, and more). Constantly looking backward is a pathway to business stagnation. With the fast pace of business, past experiences quickly lose their relevance. Eyes forward, please. Historical information is useful, but should not be the sole basis for planning future-forward growth.

Who Are You Planning for?

There is planning for you and then there is planning for others. They are different. For yourself, planning is laying out a game plan for the future, while a Business Plan for funders, venture capitalists, partners, or other audiences, is a sales document. Yes, it will contain certain elements of realistic (or semirealistic) planning, but mostly it will be a promotional tool responding to the "what they need to hear" essentials of the respective audiences. Keep your eye on the proposed readership for your presentation.

The Spectator Mode: How to Think through Everything Important

Picture yourself sitting high up in a stadium and carefully watching the goings-on down below. You are objective and somewhat removed from the direct hoopla on the field. You have no real favorites and no preconceived notion of the outcome. Instead, you are a keen observer. You can weigh every element of the game down below.

That is the spectator mode, taking a step back from anything you may be planning, weighing all aspects of the impact of your decision, and adopting a very rational, objective approach to any scenario being considered.

The spectator mode forces you to take the emotion out of your strategic planning process. In many instances, the presence and input of an impartial third party, who has no vested interest in the business, can also be a valuable sounding board for you.

Another way to achieve the enlightenment proffered by the spectator mode is to carry out your planning session away from the office at a resort or other such getaway. This successfully separates everyone involved from their desks, cell phones (no phones allowed), and ever-present daily deadlines and pressures. The only drawback to getaway planning sessions is the tendency to quickly back-burner any ideas once you get reimmersed into the daily grind at the office. Be aware of that. Resist shelving what you have so carefully decided upon at your getaway planning.

The Right Business Plan for the Right Audience

In simplest terms, a Business Plan is a snapshot of who you are, where you are in your business growth, what you want to do, why you want to do it, what will it do for you (outcomes, deliverables), why you know it will succeed, how you will get there, how long it will take you, what you need to do (action plan), and what you need to access (e.g., funding) to get you there. That's most of your generic Business Plan. But there's more.

Every Business Plan also has an "**ask**," what you are asking for from the intended reader. The "**ask**" is keynote. It dictates how your Business Plan should be tweaked specifically to your immediate audience. Funders?

Partnership opportunities? Investors? Strategic partner? Focus. Each different target reader will be searching for what interests them the most. It's that self-interest/selfish gene stuff we have been talking about at length. The most important focus in your Plan is what the **target readership needs to hear**. It's time to kowtow, big time. Here are some thoughts.

A Business Plan for traditional funders and government funders should include the following:

- Justification of the initiative, and why you are undertaking it.
- Proof of concept. Yes, there is an identified need or niche. Yes, the market is big enough. Yes, you have orders or letters of intent, or interest. Yes, the market penetration is viable, and not built on a trillion-dollar awareness-building and time-consuming campaign to educate the market.
- Risk assessment that mitigates identifiable threats. Lenders abhor risk.
- Cash flows. Include a gameplan as to how you intend to reimburse the money.
- Comfort. Remember who you are dealing with, and what you have achieved in the recent past.

A Business Plan for investors and venture funds must necessarily include the following:

- This is the big picture. Here is how the project will capture market share with a strong position.
- A really important component of the plan for investors is a stress test for return on investment (ROI). This is often one of the most important tests applied by investors.
- Here is proof of concept that there is a market interest and need.
- These are the "carrots." "With your help, this is what we all can look like downstream with leapfrogged or new products and services and building on the client base".
- **PPE**. This is how your investment will be **protected** (secured with xxx, if possible), these are the anticipated **profits**, and this is your **exit strategy** when you want to cash out (generally a sale of shares, or a public issue).

Of course, the traditional Business Plan for yourself is far more conservative since it is a roadmap for your company's growth.

- In budgeting, eliminate your "rose-colored glasses" syndrome by increasing your expected expenses and reducing your projected revenues by 50 percent. When you actually exceed your forecasts, you will be a hero.
- Alternatively, you can consider creating three budget scenarios: worst, most likely, and (OMG) best case ever.
- Generate an Action Plan based on readily achievable "Baby Steps," and with a timeline that is realizable.
- Don't make it all too easy on yourself with these planning parameters, but don't set the yardsticks so high that you will get altitude sickness trying to reach them.

Deconstructing the Business Plan: The Reader's Perspective

The Internet is overflowing with traditional Business Plan templates, which are all virtually the same, so there is no reason to regurgitate a full outline here. Mr. Google alone, in only 0.61 seconds, responds with 3.1 billion results when asked for "Business Plans" and 1.4 billion results in 0.58 seconds when asked about "Business Plan Templates." I am truly humbled by you, Mr. Google.

A business idea is just another idea. But an idea backed by proven feasibility is now a solid business opportunity worth pursuing.
                                                                    Ajaero Tony Martins

Your Business Plan is more than a collection of words and numbers. It needs to touch the reader and keep them interested and motivated to know more, and inspired to participate via whatever your "ask" might be. So, assuming you know what goes into each chapter of a Business Plan, the far more important question is "after reviewing the chapter, what does the reader now know?"

Business plan chapter	What does the reader now know?
Executive summary	• Has a basic understanding about your company/project • Wants to learn more about your business
Business description and vision	• What the business is all about, in great detail • Your goals and vision as to where the company is going in relation to the readers' vision for participating • Comfort in understanding and appreciating your roots, how you have grown the company, and your ability to spearhead the intended changes/expansion, etc.
Definition of the market	• Information about the marketplace • Competition and market share • Your market research and findings and, more importantly, what it all means • How your market research justifies the project • A clear understanding of your customer base and future clientele that the project may be targeting • Long-term "carrots" downstream
Products and services	• Your products and services, average margins and markups • Security of supply chains • Product and service competitiveness
Organization and management	• Legalities and ownership, share structure • Key management • Organigram and general organizational flow • Reporting and accountability
Marketing and sales strategy	• Who your market is • How you reach your market • Client loyalty • Brand loyalty and image recognition • Marketing strategies • Distribution channels • Competitive edge • Ability to capture additional or new market share
Financial management	• Company's financial capacity • Comfort with financial projections • Security, that is, investment protection • Ability to repay, if that is in the deal • Exit strategies
Operational plan	• Ability to deliver what the company offers in products or services • Facility management • Clear division of roles and responsibilities
Conclusions	• Your "ask" • Confirmation of your abilities and the company's • Your ideas are well thought out and researched • Risks are within reason, that is, "livable" • Long-term potential is realistic • Absence of rose-colored glasses in the Plan • Understanding of the timelines and window of opportunity

Your Business Plan Demands Third Party Due Diligence

Let others close to you play the "devil's advocate" and grill you relent-lessly on your Plan. You will be surprised how an intelligent, objective observer can pick holes in your ideas (or conversely, instill conviction and reinforce your motivation). In either case, that's what you need, because, backtracking and major shifts in your planning are costly, in money, time, and credibility.

Who can be your sounding board?

- Trusted business associates who do not have any self-interest in your project, or any real or perceived conflict of interest
- Your accountant, assuming they have skills beyond just record-keeping. Your accountant's role should generally be limited to your forecasts and number crunchings
- Fair-minded business consultants who have hands-on real-world experience in your sector, or something reasonably compatible
- Managers from your company whose future success is not tied into the realization of the project
- Anyone you have worked closely with, particularly someone who called upon you in the past for you to review their Business Plan

Who should not be your sounding board?

- Managers from your company whose future success is tied directly into the realization of the project. You need impartiality and de-tachment, and not self-interest that can skew feedback.
- Mom, Dad, cousin George, grandma, your rugby buddies … think you get it. They will be 100 percent supportive or 100 percent jeal-ous. Either way, these will be emotional reactions.
- Consultants who are super excited before they even know all the facts. They are feathering their potential work with you.
- Stereotypical lawyers who spend as much time explaining their billing structure as they do offering a semblance of advice during the initial free consultation. Ask about their fees.

The Action Plan: Moving Ahead, Step by Step

Quite often the Action Plan is integrated into the Business Plan, or is presented as a secondary document to your target audience. It can be the basis for your marketing and planning meetings. Personally, I have always preferred the Action Plan as a separate strategy paper. Why? Because with a specific target readership in mind, that is, an investor or venture group, it gave me the opportunity to meet with them once again, and, in doing so, further reinforce the Business Plan and the deliverable benefits to the funder. It also helped build the relationship. Face-to-face meetings are powerful bonding experiences.

The Action Plan is pure methodology:

- What you want to do
- What steps need to be carried out to get there
- Phases and achievable milestones broken down to "Baby Steps"
- What milestone can indicate that a step (or steps) have delivered the intended results
- What the timelines for completion are for each stage
- How progress can be measured. The quantifiable aspect is important
- How each step is part of a game plan to deliver results as proposed in the Business Plan
- Quite often Gantt charts are a vital part of Action Plans. These bar charts illustrate a project schedule and anticipated milestones across a series of timelines

Build an Exit Strategy for Yourself

Build your own expiry date into your Action Plan. Nobody is there forever.

Are you the business start-up guy or the operations guy? Assume that somewhere down the road you will get bored, or see the opportunity to sell, or be blinded by a new shiny coin on the road.

A reasonable action item will be to hire an operation CEO and allow yourself the flexibility to move on.

This Is How It Works in Real Life

I had somehow inherited a tech client who had an unabated appetite to pursue funding. Tech companies are money eating machines, particularly during their formative years, or if they are in the midst of pricey and risky research or development.

The client knew that her Business Plans and forecasts had to be tailored to her audience, and that was good. Her problem was that she was overzealous in her "customization" efforts.

Instead of working with a core Plan and adapting it to fit the intended readers, she created 12 different Business Plans and, worst of all, 12 very different financial forecasts to fit the investment criteria of each funder. Each was told a different story. She was a big believer in telling funders what she thought they wanted to hear, regardless of any confusion this might have caused between stakeholders.

The issue? As she was juggling discussions and negotiations with all these players, she started confusing what she had told to whom. This confusion, alas, extended to which Business Plans and forecasts she had presented them with. For security purposes, each Plan was named with only a number. (Leave it to a scientist, albeit a brilliant one, to dig herself into a hole.) The venture community is a small one. People talk.

I identified the most interested venture capital companies, of which there were four, and I politely discarded the rest. I then sought out any semblance of commonality between the Plans, and then created one new Business and Investment Plan that built upon a new, updated scenario for growth and diversification, responding to the PPE (protection, profit, and exit) doctrine that excites most funders. This was then presented as "new and improved," and all previous Plan versions were effectively "outdated."

In the end, funding did materialize, but the battle to re-establish credibility resulted in tougher investment terms linked with restrictive reporting and performance tracking requirements.

CHAPTER 12

Opportunities and the Shiny Coin Syndrome

Someone is sitting in the shade today because someone planted a tree a long time ago.

Warren Buffett

Look! Another Business Opportunity!

You have a game plan for your business. Someone proposes another opportunity beyond the scope of your plans, but one that has great sparkle. What do you do? Back-burner everything else to pursue the rainbow? Worried that if you don't act, it will evaporate? Possibly blinded by greed?

It is the nature of entrepreneurs to seek out and act on opportunities, but often erroneously at the expense of "the bird in the hand" business they have already built. It's a balancing act, not a belly flop from the high board into the deep end. Stay on track.

Find a Winner, Mimic a Winner

In researching an opportunity, why reinvent the wheel? If there is someone somewhere doing anything similar to the opportunity you are considering, then find out everything about them. If they were sitting across the desk, what would you want to ask them? With that in hand, call them (assuming they are not a nearby competitor). Entrepreneurs like to talk, share, and even brag a bit. Or, pretend to be an interested customer (flexible ethics, remember?). Or, visit their place of business. Just latch on to others within your sector and learn what you can from them. Learn from them. It could be the best opportunity research you will do.

The Serendipitous Origins of New Business Opportunities

Your "eureka moment" can strike you when you are humming (likely off-key) your favorite tunes in the shower or sitting at a meeting at work or a party at a friend's house, and you are doodling out of boredom. A flash of inspiration may arrive during a lengthy commute, or even, dare I say, sitting on the "throne" and focusing on nothing in particular. Seriously, the latter, often referred to as the "think tank," is a peaceful time that allows for creative brainstorming and organizing your thoughts. (Honestly, there is some stuff I cannot make up.)

The common thread here is, your mind, that is, your imagination, should be freed up to wander and explore without the constraints of "must get done" and "have to remember to." Ideas germinate when you clear your brain fog.

In effect, you really need to stop thinking too much. That can be achieved inadvertently out of boredom or downtime, or intentionally by practicing meditation and mindfulness, or just taking time for reflection. Even daydreaming. It's like changing the channel and watching The Maltese Falcon with the sound off.

Vigorous exercise frees your mind as well. When jogging through national parks, I would often get a burst of some idea or a fragment of a vague notion and would frantically seek out someone who had something I could scribble a note on.

The majority of business ideas come from your workplace or traditional stimuli, such as trade shows, hobbies, media, intentional research, and copycatting others. However, a high percentage show up by chance, and those tend to be some of the more innovative and "why not try this" business prospects.

Interestingly enough, lovemaking is often cited as an activity that encourages the creative flow of new entrepreneurial opportunities. The release of endorphins is a natural stimulant. So what do you think about during sex? An app? A new clothing line? Starting an urban professional coffee bar?

And while we are on the topic of "passion," being passionate about an idea or opportunity is one of the key drivers that encourages you to follow through with the opportunity, or at least until you arrive at a "go/no-go" decision as to whether or not to pursue a business idea. Keep in mind that idea could be for a new venture or a growth strategy for an existing enterprise. Passion is not just for start-up junkies.

Research, Research, Research. Then Do It Again

Business, more than any other occupation, is a continual calculation, an instinctive exercise in foresight.

Henry R. Luce

Don't just believe what you want to hear. The danger of market research is sometimes continuing the investigative process until you find someone or some source that tells you it's a good idea, which is what you wanted to hear in the first place. A validation. Twenty sources say no, three say maybe, one says terrific. "See I told you it was a great opportunity!"

Market research slows the process of jumping into an opportunity, be that a new venture, strategic growth of your business, or growth by acquisition or merger.

The well-established cornerstones of market research are: trade shows, surveys, focus groups, customer satisfaction questionnaires, Internet blitz, telephone surveys or even focus groups. Most work, but the best market research needs a more edgy, in-your-face approach. Here are a few:

- Field research. Introducing a new coffee line? Go to where customers buy coffee and offer samples. Outside coffee shops (I like this one). Inside grocery stores. At events.
- Be odd and innovative. It works. A small business client wanted to get feedback on a new massage therapy franchise she wanted to launch, to get media attention and to garner new customers. I suggested she set up a massage table and relief station in the parking lot of a major retailer. It was different enough that people stopped to chat and provide input while they received a free mini-massage. It worked wonderfully.
- Talk to indirect competitors, defined as someone in your business but geographically far enough away that they are not direct

competition. So picture yourself across the desk from them, and you have 10 minutes to ask them anything. What would you want to know? Prepare judiciously in advance for your calls. And, by the way, after you introduce yourself, make sure you flatter them about their website, business, ads, anything, whereby flattery, sincere or not, will open the conversational floodgates. I believe that's called flexible ethics, yes?

- Do not wear rose-colored glasses which make everything look great. Business reality is often less so, and you need to prepare yourself to seriously consider the negative or dark side of market research findings.

Market research is critical in any decision-making process. Don't shortchange it, or dismiss any red flags that pop up.

What Does Market Research Actually Tell You?

Just carrying out the research is half the job. You have collected an assortment of brain dump input. Great. But now you need to ask yourself how any of this applies directly to the opportunity you were researching?

- Eliminate those who were wildly enthusiastic or, at the other end of the spectrum, the curmudgeons. The extremists do you little good as their impartiality is tainted by whatever.
- Seek commonality. After enough input, you will start to see (or hear) the same type of feedback. Those are the ones you want. When you see commonality, you will know your market research has succeeded.
- Discard any findings not directly related to your research goals as they tend to muddy the waters and distract you. Stay on topic.
- Consumer validation can be achieved through the use of Mailchimp surveys (www.mailchimp.com). They have proven to be a successful tool for garnering direct customer feedback. There are numerous platforms you can use besides Mailchimp.

- Above all, let the market research findings direct your decision making. After all, this invaluable input has been gleaned from role models, direct and indirect competition, research, prospective customers, or existing clients. So, listen!

The "Funneling Down" Process of Screening Opportunities

Information accumulated during research can tend to be overwhelming. The sheer number of inputs during your exploration and planning process will likely weigh you down with not only tons of market intelligence, but also often findings and advice that contradict each other. This alone often acts as a huge roadblock for entrepreneurs.

The "**Funneling Down**" **Process** is a valuable tool for sorting information. It is a way to handle large amounts of bits and pieces and allows you to sort out the valuable from the fluff or worthless.

Basically, it implies loading everything into an information/input funnel, and study the results, taking the best and most logical material that exits the bottom of the funnel.

To deal with the mass of input, what I have traditionally done is as follows:

1. Review everything I have gathered.
2. Discard the irrelevant.
3. Discard the motherhood and fluff that tells you nothing.
4. Divide up the findings into bite-size portions, by topic.
5. Insert them into digital files. You can use hard copy and simply set up a series of large envelopes, one for each research parameter.
6. Now you can focus on one research outcome at a time.

Assessing Risk

With any opportunity, there are risks you can control, and then there are risks that are beyond your direct control, but can nonetheless impact your business, and any opportunity you might be researching. For those you can control, develop some mitigating strategies to deal with them. For the unmanageable ones, ask yourself "what if." If your response indicates they can be serious detriments or even death blows, then walk away. The key ones are as follows:

Controllable risks	Unmanageable risks
Target markets	The economy
Marketing	Politics
Financial needs	Currency fluctuations
Technology	Competition beyond your ability to compete
Pricing, margins	Proprietary technology advancements
Market preferences	Global disruptions (war, pandemics, trade wars, and other major events.)

There is another chapter in this book that deals with "Strengths, Weaknesses, Opportunities, and Threats" (SWOT) analysis, which also represents a viable risk assessment tool.

Avoid Group Decision Making

With the understanding that everyone has their own agenda and is fixated on their own self-interest, the more people you bring to the decision-making table, the more diverse the input will be, and the more difficult any decisions will become.

Keep it simple. Work only with those whose opinion and counsel you trust and value. You don't want a group of "yes" people, and you certainly don't want anyone whose input serves their own personal or business ambitions.

Setting a Value for an Opportunity Is an Artform

Valuations are a useful tool when acquiring a business (growth by acquisition), buying or selling your business, or negotiating with an investor or partner. However, it is a "black art." There are various valuation methodologies and the outcomes can differ tremendously. Valuations are often driven by self-interest, that is, whomever is paying for the valuation, so, if it's not you, then beware. A reasonable valuation is a 'compromise', accepted by both sides, but not a 'true joy' to either the buyer or the seller.

There are several **valuation approaches**. Each has its strengths and weaknesses.

- **Asset Approach**—This simple methodology uses the value based on the cost of replacing the net assets of the business, both tangible and intangible. The danger here is that some methods discount assets to fire sale values. Others dismiss intangibles such as goodwill.
- **Income Approach**—This utilizes the value based on anticipated future earnings and benefits. As you can imagine, this is highly subjective.
- **Market Approach**—This approach commonly uses multiples of EBITDA (Earnings Before Interest, Taxes, Depreciation, and Amortization) and revenues based on a history of similar business sales. The results are generally averaged out. The inherent danger here is that businesses with high revenues and slim profits show diversely different valuations once multiples are applied, and vice versa.

    Multiples of revenues and EBITDA used in valuations are generally cited as a range, with buyers using the lowest multiples and sellers using the highest. A valuation done by a buyer will definitely not be the same as one done by a seller. Some valuations include future earnings; others are more conservative and do not.

To say that business valuations are a precise science is a myth. It is a pseudo-science, really.

I have seen ivory tower accounting and consulting firms produce huge and costly valuation reports using complex formulae, with the reports and the results being almost incomprehensible to the negotiating parties, and the eventual agreed-upon price being scribbled on a Post-it note passed between the buyer and seller.

Find a valuation firm you can trust using one simple question; how many of their valuation reports led to business sales or acquisitions within a reasonable percentage of what they had delivered as a value for the business? That is the only way to separate the good from the poor valuation experts.

An Example of a Business Valuation Model Using the Income and Market Approaches

The objective of the Fair Market Value (FMV)/Business Valuation Report is to provide a third party with a valuation of a commercial enterprise, at a specific time, for the purposes of delivering an impartial financial assessment of the FMV of the business, within the guidelines of a typical "Disclaimer Note."[1]

A FMV is a logical and timely process that employs existing revenue and pretax (EBITDA) profit multiples,[2] as established by industry experts including BizMiner and BIZCOMPS,[3] who have compiled the data and multiples from thousands of business sales throughout North America.

FMV is often cited within a report as a "range," to accommodate for any minor fluctuations in data. In order to arrive at an FMV, the process itself can follow a proprietary[4] multi-stage analysis similar to the following model:

---

[1]Disclaimer Note: The Fair Market/Business Valuation may not purport to make any statements regarding the strength of any Letters Patent, trademarks, or other legal issues, or litigation, or issues not disclosed during the course of a Valuation Analysis, or the accuracy of forecasts and budgets presented by the seller, or ensuing errors and omissions. It generally makes no warranties and representations on conclusions drawn solely from information and financial projections supplied by the seller.

[2]"Revenue valuation multiple" is a typical tool used to appraise businesses based on market comparison to similar companies that have sold in the recent past. The valuator can multiply the subject business revenues or net sales by the revenue valuation multiple. The result is the estimate of the business market value. The same principle can be used by multiplying "EBITDA" by another set of "EBITDA multiples" available as industry standards based on past business sale experiences in North America. See http://www.valuadder.com/

[3]http://www.sec.gov/info/edgar/siccodes.htm; http://www.bizminer.com/cart/default .php; http://valuationresources.com/Misc/ValuationMultiples.htm; http://www .collin.edu/sbdc/docs/Business-Valuation-Methods.pdf; IBISWorld. "Industry Research Reports." http://www.ibisworld.com/industry/home.aspx?partnerid=Valuatio nResources, (date accessed June 10, 2020).

[4]Developed by Jay Silverberg, Author and Business Consultant.

Stage	Description and purpose
Business review	Generate a review of the highlights of the existing business: how they operate, how they fit into the marketplace, competition analysis, etc.
Asset sale versus equity sale	Determine whether this is intended to be a purchase of the assets only of the business or the equity (common shares) of the business. This makes a difference in how the FMV is generated.
Financial review	Present a synopsis of the existing financial performance of the existing business, based on historical and current financial statements.
Nonrecurring items	Identify items that are nonrecurring in the profit and loss statement, that is, one-time losses (or gains), disposal of assets, draws, and personal expenses charged to the business by the current owner.
Normalized EBITDA	Using the nonrecurring items, adjust the profit and loss statements to reflect a condition of "normal," that is, what the existing business can deliver in EBITDA. The FMV based on the true earnings potential (normalized) is one standard method of working to arrive towards a FMV.
Balance sheet	List all current assets (inventory, accounts receivable, cash, etc.), depreciated fixed assets (buildings, equipment, etc.), current liabilities (taxes, accounts payable, etc.), and long-term liabilities (leases, mortgages, loans, etc.)
Fixed assets review	This is threefold: (1) identify the items that go with the business, or stay with the existing owner (i.e., shareholders loans and other items may not be part of the "deal"); (2) review fixed assets and their depreciated value, and assess whether that might be too low, that is, written off greater than current market value; (3) discern if the balance contains any items such as goodwill or start-up costs, and whether they are still valid for consideration.
Future plans	If the buyer has future plans for the expansion or diversification of the business, these should be identified.
Future-forward profit and loss	Carry out a 3-year "going forward" estimate of revenues and EBITDA. Any future plans may receive very minor (if any at all) consideration in the valuation.
Averaging (weighting) of revenues	Using a statistical model, giving weight (% out of 100%) to both historical and future revenues, with future revenues receiving very minor consideration, average the revenues and arrive at an annual average. This represents the average revenues the business can likely generate for the new owner.

Stage	Description and purpose
Averaging (weighting) of EBITDA	Same as above, but dealing with EBITDA.
SWOT – Strengths, Weaknesses, Opportunities, Threats	Looking at a number of factors of the business (SWOT), decrease the valuation by an appropriate percentage. This is done to present as conservative an FMV as is reasonably possible.
Applying industry SIC/NAICS code[5] multiples	Using industrywide (such as BizComps[6]) multiples applied to specific business types, identify the multiples to be applied to the averaged revenues, as determined in the previous stage.
Comparable transactions	Carry out a search for comparable sales of businesses in the region. If any are identified, review the available information.
FMV using revenues and multiples	Carry out an FMV ('Fair Market Value') of the business, based on the above process results, and based on revenues.
FMV using EBITDA and multiples	Carry out an FMV ('Fair Market Value') of the business, based on the above process results and based on EBITDA.
Final FMV statement	Average the results of the above revenues and EBITDA FMV calculations, and deliver a range of estimated Fair Market Value of the business. The FMV is now a 'snapshot' of the business at a very specific time and stage of development.

---

[5]The Standard Industrial Classification (SIC) is a government system for classifying industries by a four-digit code. Established in 1937, it is being supplanted by the six-digit North American Industry Classification System (NAICS code), which was released in 1997; however, many still use the SIC codes (http://en.wikipedia.org/wiki/SIC_codes).
[6]ValuSource. "BIZCOMPS." https://www.valusource.com/products/business-appraiser-databases/bizcomps/, (date accessed June 10, 2020).

Let's Get Personal. "Go/No-Go" Is Strictly Your Decision

Sometimes what looks like brilliance is really just guts.

Dan Waldscmidt

Ultimately, you will arrive at a time to make a "go/no-go" decision. Do you proceed or walk away? Your decision should be governed by a series of criteria that you yourself need to establish. It's personal. It may include any or all of the following:

- Is it affordable?
- Does the market research validate the opportunity to the degree to which I am comfortable?
- If it fails, can I (or my business) afford the capital loss?
- Are there controllable market or industry trends I can deal with?
- Are there unmanageable market or industry trend risks that are "too close for comfort"?
- Am I looking at all this through rose-colored glasses?
- Do the numbers make sense, or is the bottom line too slim to be an assured positive cash flow?
- Are there threats that I cannot control? Outside my ability to change (including pandemics, war, trade wars, and currency fluctuations)?
- Are there any issues of the business I am not comfortable with or outside my areas of expertise, e.g., markets, production, supply chains, staffing?
- If I give each of these items a score of 1 to 10, how does the opportunity stack up?
- Finally weighing all these factors, should I proceed?

This Is How It Works in Real Life

ABC Company had a techie-winner product. Their sales skyrocketed. Then they went bankrupt. Why? Growing too fast made their banks nervous. They limited ABC's line until they had more of a historical track record. Venture funds were delirious and greedy and tried to oust the founders. A battle ensued. Shareholders became suspicious, with predict-able infighting for control. And the founders, well, in their euphoric state of 'new riches' wealth, surrounded themselves with "yes men" and then became personally unreachable. They bought expensive toys. Cash flow dried up. R&D stopped because the thinking was they had a command-ing edge (even as competitors began to reverse engineer and improve on ABC's technology). They had even started looking at new businesses be-fore they stabilized the growth of their existing company.

You cannot ever lose sight of the fact that your "edge," whatever that might be, has granted you a favored position in the marketplace. It could be your technology, products, services, or your own personal drive and abilities.

Focus. Don't get distracted or sidetracked. Any time and resources employed for new ideas and opportunities detract from your time and focus you are devoting to your existing business. It will cost you.

And try not to get bored or complacent with your business. The ten-dency for "start-up junkies" is to get bored. I admit to being one. Our minds wander. We seek out new adventures.

Try to restrain your entrepreneurial wanderlust.

CHAPTER 13

Communications and Networking Involves Talking AND Listening. Sounds So Easy, Right?

I've learned that people will forget what you said, people will forget what you did, but people will never forget how you made them feel.

Maya Angelou

Communication: You Can Talk, Right?

Right. We all know how to talk, but not all of us know how to communicate.

Communication is the ability to get a point across or stimulate action on the part of the listener. Action like closing a sale. Communication needs to have a purpose, and "yes," communicating can be a learned talent.

Business communication is exchanging information in order to promote an organization's goals, objectives, purpose, and activities, as well as increase profits within the company.

Wikipedia

Practice. Take acting classes. Learn to fake conversations if you must, where you need to show interest, pleasant surprise, and even downright enlightenment. Make the co-conversationalist feel important, smart, and special. Make effective communication second nature to you.

(Actually, if communication was taught starting in kindergarten, there would be far fewer brawls in the recess playground, don't you think? Suggest it to your school board.)

Communication Tactics: Meeting and Influencing People

It's too tempting to jump into conversations or try to control an exchange by talking about yourself (or your company, or your personal opinion on whatever) and making yourself the center of attention. Try hard to avoid that. It's self-defeating. It deflates any rapport that has been built between you. It begs the old adage "just shut up and listen!" Restrain yourself.

That said, there are a series of tactics you can employ. Practice using them. They work. These simple strategies will help you get to "yes," which is likely what you are after. Yes to buy, yes to try, yes to whatever is important to you. Some of these are outstanding examples of integrating flexible ethics into your people skills.

- Never complain about anything. Assume nobody cares, because they don't. Get over the disappointment. However, if the other party complains, be ever so compassionate, even empathetic, for example, "That happened to me once too. It was terrible. It must have shaken you." We humans crave sympathy.
- Listen. It is probably one of the toughest skills to learn. Hold back. Wait for your conversation entry point. Let the other(s) do most of the talking, especially at the beginning of a conversation. That also gives you the opportunity to figure out where the conversation is going, and deflect it carefully toward your own objectives.
- Listening is not enough. You must hear what is being said. You may be expected to respond, and there may even be a 'test' later, so listen up!
- Assume the other party is always right. Respect their perspective, even if it is diametrically opposite your own. It doesn't matter. Play the game.
- Remember names. The expression "even dogs have names" is a cruel reminder that communication needs to be intimate.

- Be humble. It empowers the other party.
- If you are pushing for results or action, and you detect resistance, back off. Try again later.
- Guide the other person to take ownership, for example, "You know, I think that could work for us."
- You cannot build yourself up on your competitor's shortcomings. People get offended by that. If you must, compliment your competitor before you tear into them.
- Be happy. Make others happy. Stay upbeat. Avoid conversations that elicit furrowed brows, e.g., world problems and global plights.
- Avoid any talk about politics, religion, diet and sex. While this is an old piece of advice, I have witnessed communication painfully shut down like a floodgate when the parties broach any of these hypersensitive topics. People form "opinion camps," and communication simply stops. People keep talking, yes, but nobody actually says anything.

Learn to Play Nice

Keep lines of communication open, regardless of the relationship. Being nasty may feel good, but it's a very temporary pleasure, with a heavy potential price tag later on. My mother used to say, "If you have nothing nice to say, don't say anything." So, play nice.

Sometimes playing nice is tough, especially if there is any animosity or disrespect toward the other party. Just imagine that the other person is possibly harboring the same attitude when communicating with you. It's more like a polite standoff, with both parties hopefully walking away with what they are seeking from the other. So, again, play nice. Hey, business is a game, remember?

The Broken Telephone Nightmare

Remember the kid's game where you sat in a circle and the first person whispered something to the next person, and around the circle it went until it came out at the end as something totally different and unrecognizable? Business communication is worse.

The situations I have found myself in by believing third-hand information were almost comical. One of my partners was the worst in that he exaggerated everything. A displeased client was "ready to sue us." A missed opportunity was a "death blow for our company."

I learned that anything other than first-hand information directly from the source was ambiguous and grossly misrepresented, and often sent me into an apoplectic tailspin. I don't think there was any intended malice. People simply hear what they want or need to hear. Go to the prime source, always.

Skating, the Art of Empty but Effective Responses

Avoiding the subject or switching the focus of a discussion is a true art form. It denotes responding without answering. We see this in politics, but it is amateurish and often comically obvious. However, in business it is a critical skill.

- Question: "How many employees do you have?"
  Answer: "We have a team of contracted, virtual employees."
- Question: "How many years have you been in business?"
  Answer: "I have been involved in this sector for 20 years."
- Question: "Is your company certified to environmental standards?"
  Answer: "We practice great care in all areas where there can be an impact on the environment."

That's skating. Pay attention and don't get caught off guard or speechless. Here are a few tips:

- Repeat or rephrase the question. It sounds like you are doing so to make sure you understand it, but really it's a stalling tactic to give you time to think of an appropriate response. (Kids have perfected this technique. Just ask "Who broke this?")
- Shift focus off yourself. You can do so by saying, for example, "I understand why that is important to you" or an empathetic diversion to that effect.

- Avoid bravado. It's like playing "chicken" and, even in winning, you lose.
- Cede control. Whatever the other party's concerns or objections might be, agree with them, then proceed to defend or alter their position. By agreeing with them, you are empowering them. People like that.
- Body language is also important. That means maintaining eye contact and not fidgeting or crossing your arms in a defensive pose. You would be astounded how simple body language can build or diminish your image in other person's eyes.

Skating involves compromising yourself, and you need to weigh the consequences of bending versus scoring. It's personal. I have always looked at compromise as part of playacting my business persona role, so I have never really had an issue with it. That is one perspective you may want to consider.

Parent-to-Parent Communications: Talk to, Not at People

There are three identified levels of communication, namely parent to parent, parent to child, and child to parent. The only one of any consequence in business is parent to parent.

- Speak to others as if they are your equals. Even if you feel they are above or beneath you, treat them as equals.
- Deal with people how you would like to be dealt with.
- Avoid talking down to people. That is parent to child thinking and is sure to get a negative response and a closed mind.
- If you are being talked down to, raise the adult bar in the conversation. Show knowledge and insight that enhances you in the eyes of the annoying belittler.
- Stay the painful course if you want that contract and cope, cope, cope. Again, business is just a game, but often a game of nerves and strategies too.

Getting Away with Finesse Intimidation

The Theory of Intimidation states that the results a person achieves are inversely proportionate to the degree to which he is intimidated.

Robert Ringer

There are degrees of intimidation, from the blatant and transparent bullying to the coercion by finesse.

- The **takeaway** implies offering to tactfully walk away from a deal in order to get a stubborn client to meet your price or terms. You can do this even if you are somewhat desperate for the work, but cannot live with what the client dictates. That's finesse intimidation. More often than not, the "takeaway" brings the parties back to the table.
- The second is **painting into a corner**, which simply implies making a statement the client cannot argue with. For example, in charity telemarketing, the caller says, "You don't really want to see those kids in Polonia go all winter without shoes, right?" or the telemarketer hawking an investment saying, "You like to make money, don't you?" I never liked doing this, or getting it done to me. That's just bullying and insulting. Clients will take offense.
- If your intimidation style or strategy is presenting ultimatums, then the advice here is be prepared to follow through with them.

Bluffing

The best way to describe bluffing is "pretending," like building a start-up website or brochure that makes you look well established, or talking to clients about your "team" (i.e., Mom, Dad, Woofy), or even embellishing testimonials (which few ever check, by the way).

When dealing with people, watch for poker-type "tells," like body language and eye movement, etc. You can identify when your audience is vulnerable, and to what degree you can bluff.

Bluffing also implies playing a hand that you are not holding, but hoping others believe you are. How's your poker face?

Then there's the extreme, which involves **extreme flexible ethics** that I am not comfortable with. Someone I know was promoting English language training in China and implied they were part of Oxford University. They included the Oxford name and logo on their material. In fact, they were simply using the Oxford dictionary as a training resource. Status is so very important in China, and the ruse worked well, but I am certain people were hurt with this level of deceit.

Sales Manipulating to "Yes"

I've always loved the idea of not being what people expect me to be.
Dita Von Teese

Manipulating sales tactics can be somewhat coarse, some even say "mercenary," but they exist because they still work. My suggestion is to review and understand these approaches and then think about how they can possibly be modified to fit your own sensibilities. I don't ascribe to these, but take from them what you can. There are lessons here.

- **Make a statement**, possibly in the form of a question that has no answer, such as, "You do want to buy that new Tesla, don't you?" (Duh)
- **Sell, then add some snob appeal/exclusivity to close the deal**, for example, "It's obvious that you are interested in the proposition, but I can only offer it to and work with one group, so..."
- **Fear then relief**, an example might be , "Y2K (remember that?) can wipe out all your computer records, but we have a solution."
- **Compliments** (real or insincere) get people to let their guards down.
- **Returning favors,** by saying something like "Remember when I covered for you, well I need you now."
- **Illusion of choice,** where the manipulator instills some urgency for a decision. An example might be, a limited-time offer or a brief window of opportunity to act.
- **Guilt.** My mother's favorite. (I don't think any of us need examples.)

- **Building a comfort level and a bond** (again, real or insincere) that makes others feel happy to deal with you.
- **A "foot in the door"** is a classic manipulation, whereby the original "ask" or opportunity offered is reasonably small, free, or very attractive and does not represent a huge commitment when couched properly. It then leads to a bigger obligation downstream, like "Join the wine-of-the-month club for free, and then only buy ten more cases a year, at a huge member's discount, obviously."
- **Make it memorable**, for example, "Your children will thank you."
- **Ridiculously honest plea** (again, real or fictitious). Interestingly, this works and puts guilt onto the client, by uttering something like "If I don't fill my quota, I may lose my job. Anything you can do to help?"
- **Time constraints** and deadlines by dangling a carrot like "This proposal is good for 30 days. We can price-protect for that period."
- **Exploiting a weakness.** When you know your target, and what their issues might be, you can poke a finger in the wound. This is pretty low, but from a manipulation aspect, appealing to a person's or company's Achilles' heel is devastatingly effective.
- **Peer pressure**, for example, "All your competitors are subscribing to this software management tool," (true or selectively true) implying the people you are speaking with will recede back to the Stone Age if they do not keep up.
- **Promises you never made.** This is rampant with telemarketing charities, and goes something like "Thank you for your generous contribution last year to the blind ice hockey association." What?
- **Always dominate any interaction.** Major presenters and hucksters live and breathe this technique. Watch them and you will see they rarely let anyone else speak, and certainly do not allow anyone to control the dialogue.

As you can guess, manipulation can get nasty. They exude flexible ethics. Use these techniques wisely and judiciously. It takes a certain mindset to carry them out shamelessly, except if you are like my ex-partner, in which case, fill your boots.

Networking Is the Art of "Applied Communications"

Networking isn't how many people you know, it's how many people know you.

Amit Kalantri

Networking is a two-way street for communicating with groups (two or more people) in a constructive, two-way dialogue that includes the unselfish sharing of information, contacts, and opportunities. You need to offer as much as you expect to get. Develop trust and respect. Do favors, and expect favors in return. In short, there needs to be something in it for all parties.

But if you are in a networking situation and someone whips out a business card and asks you if you need a new car or insurance before you even introduce yourself, then you need to run away in the middle of their sales pitch as there will be nothing in the networking for you (except maybe a 5 percent discount on that new minivan of your dreams).

Where do you network? Everywhere. Trade shows, conferences, parties, Chambers of Commerce get-togethers, association meetings. I have even networked in hotel washrooms during conference breaks. No, don't ask.

There is no room in networking for "takers" and "predators." Pretty simple. You get what you give.

Call it a clan, call it a network, call it a tribe, call it a family. Whatever you call it, whoever you are, you need one.

Jane Howard

Here are some tips that need to become second nature to your performance in a group opportunity. You will notice, incidentally, that the term "performance" is used here because, for many people, networking is uncomfortable and needs to be learned and practiced to be effective. If networking is a foreign and awkward concept for you, then theater classes would be most helpful, where you can learn to be an effective and compelling "schmoozer."

So how do you network like a pro? Here are some network "moves" to try. They work.

- The room for whatever event you are attending is your stage. Work it. Join into groups. Make your presence felt.
- Be a "princess." Arrive late. Be eccentric. Wear those red sneakers. Be memorable. Get remembered.
- Find people who can be directly or indirectly useful to you and build relationships. Remember, "indirectly" refers to those multipliers who can facilitate introductions to people or companies who can prove useful for you. This is part of the premise of 'using people'.
- Above all, listen! Don't be the showoff or loudmouth. Be respectfully attentive. Hold back on your compunction to start pitching.
- Create an "elevator pitch" that can be delivered in 30 to 45 seconds. Within that short time frame, pack in who you are and what you do for clients. Possibly name-drop as well.
- Give as much as you get. You are far more likely to get referrals if you have offered leads in exchange. And maybe do so first before they do.
- Always be marketing as part of your networking. Have you noticed that realtors always wear their name tags everywhere, and on every occasion? That is ultimate marketing.

Guan Xi, the Chinese Art of Networking

It's not what you know, it's who you know. In China the wheels of business are lubricated with guanxi.

Will Kenton

The Chinese business culture goes back thousands of years. Chinese traders were doing deals and building business relationships while Egypt's New Kingdom was collapsing, Greece was going into the Dark Ages, Rome was just seven hills with a few hamlets, the Celtic migrations were beginning in Europe, and North America was inhabited by diverse

Indian cultures.[1] Okay, I think you get it. It's been around forever. It must work, right?

Chinese business practices formed the very foundation for commerce. It was, and still is called, "Guan Xi." It brings together personal and business relationship building and the personal connections of trading favors, and being able to call upon one another to do so. It is decidedly reciprocal.

Today, Guan Xi is the cornerstone of social and business networking, built on friendships and trustworthiness. Those with relationships feel an obligation to do business with their "friends."

The intrinsic danger of Guan Xi is that anyone outside their direct sphere is fair game. We see this primarily when North Americans deal with China. Simply placing orders for yet more products made in China is just business, not Guan Xi. So it does not really command the respectful parameters of doing business with friends. People complain about Chinese suppliers, but they are simply suppliers and nothing else. Guan Xi networking demands more.

The lesson here is clear. In any of your dealings, build relationships before you build business. Utilize Guan Xi as a successful model for developing all your business connections and networks. This applies everywhere and with everyone you do business, locally, nationally, and internationally.

This Is How It Works in Real Life

At a networking event, I had met the owner of a large-scale plastics injection molding company. I zeroed in on him as a potential client.

What did he manufacture? Garbage cans. Lots of them. I listened to him speak with great pride about his business. I actually strained to find questions to ask him. What kind of garbage cans? How many sizes? Colors? Employees? Revenues? House brand or private label? Use of recycled or virgin plastic? Distribution channels? Margins?

---

[1]Native American Netroots. June 30, 2020. "Ancient America: 3,000 Years Ago." http://nativeamericannetroots.net/diary/994, (date accessed June 20, 2020).

He was enthralled. Nobody had really shown this kind of interest in his business, or asked him such pointed questions. In turn, he was most receptive to find out more about my business development consulting firm. A synergistic relationship was building.

I slept well that night, with garbage bins instead of sheep jumping over the fence. He became a long-term client and I even convinced him to start producing lawn ornament pink flamingos (and other garden ornaments like gnomes and fountains), of which he sold millions. But he still cranked out his beloved garbage cans.

CHAPTER 14

Never Surrender Control. You Earned It. You Keep It

You can't always control the wind, but you can control your sails.
Anthony Robbins

Emotional Detachment Is Control

There are two worlds you likely live in, the real world of family, friends, kids, and cute puppy dogs, and then there is the business world. The latter is your alternate universe, kind of like that Star Trek episode with evil Kirk and villainous Spock.

The business world should be pretty well void of emotions and emotional attachments. Your so-called "friends" in business will often unceremoniously dump you for others who can better serve their needs (or vice versa), so don't expect them to be on your Christmas card list forever. That includes employees, partners, and investors.

Don't expect forever accolades. Don't think anyone you meet or work with in business will remember you once you are of little or no use to them. I had a client in the lighting industry who lost a contract with a very long-term customer over $0.05 a fixture. Learn from it. Toughen up.

If you cannot control your emotions, you cannot control your money.
Warren Buffett

Emotion versus Passion

Emotion is often considered a detriment in business decision-making. It can taint the entrepreneur's perception of the choices or issues and can render a decision based on highly charged personal predilections, or the individual's tendencies to be color-blind.

Passion, on the other hand, is a driving force in business, risk-taking, and opportunity development. It is infectious to everyone surrounding you. However, it can also cede control and detachment by virtue of the sparkly rose-colored glasses you may be wearing. Get those shades off. Maintain control.

Emotion in business often has a negative undertone, while passion is perceived as quite positive. Business demands a balance between emotion and passion. Not an easy task, but striking a healthy balance provides you with exceptional insight, sensitivity, and intuition in everything you do. You need both of these strong-willed and noble drivers to help make great decisions and to control your business environment.

Micromanaging Is Not Surrendering Control

I have always been a devout micromanager. My personal modus operandi is to never let go of your role as the driving force of your business. Sure, it's great to delegate, but stay on top of everything. You will be accused of micromanaging or second guessing others, but it's your business, right? The assumption that everything is simply running along smoothly and you can take a more hands-off approach is naïve, lazy, and lethal.

Entrepreneurs are often hoarders, treating their businesses like babies, nurturing and loving their businesses to death. Experience has shown me that is not a terrible business philosophy. I have seen numerous business owners who have "over-delegated" to the point of losing control.

Many entrepreneurs adhere to the philosophy of "letting go," that is, relinquishing control including certain levels of decision making to others. The majority of "experts" preach that letting go allows the business to thrive and frees up more of the owner's time to other activities, including higher level strategic planning. My advice to you is "balance".

You only lose what you cling to.

Gautama Buddha

The degree of delegating control is obviously a personal issue hinging on the entrepreneur's comfort level in doing so, confidence in the "team," a feeling that the business is ready to be partially run by others, and the desire of the owner(s) for more time to focus on other issues and opportunities. It's very much a personal choice.

So, how do you know when you have lost control? When you need to ask your people, "How the hell did that happen?" or "How come we did not know that?"

Compromise and Downloading Control

The answer may be in "compromise." Be selective in what control you download and hoard the aspects of your business that are important to you and are fun. Don't forget the fun bits.

Further, the prudent entrepreneur will generate a priority list for the business. What aspects of the business do you want to grow? What are the challenges and potential roadblocks that the business is encountering? Then select which ones are high on your skill sets, and find people to handle the rest.

It is important to know your limits as well. As great a multitasker as you may be, we all have our limits. If you spread yourself too thin and devote your full energy to everything you do, something will suffer. Even Superman had his Kryptonite. Weaknesses prevail when we overreach.

The ability to concentrate is another factor for consideration. I can multitask with tons of distractions. I do my best work watching old movie reruns like "The Forbidden Planet" or "African Queen." One of my ex-partners, however, could not focus on more than one matter at a time, and even then, needed to be in a soundproof and distraction-free environment to focus. Bubble Boy was his nickname. So your ability to simultaneously deal effectively with the areas of your retained responsibility is contingent on your power to multi-concentrate.

Budgeting: Control Your Numbers

Control your cash. Stick to your core business. Know your numbers.
                                                    Marcus Lemonis

Staying on top of your numbers is part of control. There are two standards for budgeting, namely number crunching for yourself and budgeting for others (funders, investors).

- Forecasting for yourself takes into account every conceivable cost and scenario and is as realistic as possible. Plan for the worst, but hope for the best. Exceeding your revenues and profit forecasts is actually a thrill.
- Now, as far as budgeting for others, always make sure you demonstrate payback potential, paying out extra management fees, delivering healthy margins, ability to buy back shares, and any other investment criteria funders use as yardsticks.
- "Figures don't lie, but liars figure" really reflects the trend to get creative in budgeting. When you see a budget with skyrocketing revenues in years 3 or 4 or 5, you just know they are inventive. Nobody can realistically predict that far down the road.

Stay Healthy to Control

You cannot run your business if you do not have the strength and stamina to do so. A healthy body (or a facsimile thereof) and a clear mind are crucial to performing in business. Find the time for balance because any imbalance may itself become a source of anxiety. Exercise your body and mind. That includes meditation at work, breaks, and maintaining a healthy work–life balance for you and your people.

Your Personality Dictates Your Ability to Control and Detach

What you are made of, that is, your traits, habits, and abilities, are clear indicators of your resourcefulness to control your venture, and your capacity to delegate and detach. Who you are, your very makeup, equates to your ability to provide the kind of oversight and authority you need to start, run, and grow your business. Which of the good and bad traits do you take ownership of?

And assuming nobody is perfect, how can you work to shift any of the traits from the "bad" column to the "good" one? (You will notice that the good and bad traits in each line item are contradictory opposites of the same characteristic trait, i.e., yin and yang.)

Good traits	Bad traits
Leadership, decisive	Follower
Sensitive	Uncaring
Flexible	Inflexible, regimented
Resilient	Rigid
Stamina	Tires quickly, easily discouraged
Patient	Anxious
Ability	Bluff
Drive	Restrained, lack of initiative
Ambition	Greedy
Open	Self-centered
Amicable, sociable	Contained
Empathetic	Poor listener
Determined	Desperate
Self-motivated	Acts out of necessity
Dreamer	Overreaching
Extrovert	Introvert
Hungry	Complacent
Not wealthy	Fat and happy
Spontaneous	Deliberative
Creative	Copycat
Innovative	Fearful
Happy	Malcontent, complainer
Dynamic	Pushy
Confident, secure	Unsure
Well rounded	Narrow scope of expertise
Experienced in this business	Novice
Willing to share	Hoarder
Networker	One-way networker, taker
Resilient	Vindictive
Fearless	Reckless
Renegade	Outlaw

Good traits	Bad traits
Flexible ethics master	Unscrupulous
Disciplined	Sporadic
Proud	Pompous
Calm	Nervous, jumpy
Calculated risk-taker	Know-it-all
Humor	Cold, unfeeling
Domineering	Overpowering
Persuasive	Overbearing
Strong willed	Stubborn
Intuitive	Unspontaneous
Perspicacious	Unobservant
Caring	Callous
Principled	Immoral
Rational	Irrational

Failing Does Not Label You a Failure

Failure does not intimate that you are a failure. Most say failure is a learning experience, but, nonetheless, it is painful. Entrepreneurs see failure as a personal defeat, forgetting that business should never be personal. Failure is not the opposite of success.

This Is How It Works in Real Life

The one characteristic that was common to all my business ventures was my passion. It was passionate curiosity that nurtured my interest in the opportunity. It was passionate knowledge-seeking that led me through researching every facet. It was passionate attention to detail that led me through business planning and strategic development. It was passionate presentations, dialogue, and networking that sold others on the long-term payback and potential.

It was inspirational passion that kept me going through the start-up phase generally fraught with problems and roadblocks. It was a passion steeped in satisfaction watching the opportunity materialize, go live, and take on a life of its own. And, finally, it was the passion of yet new opportunities that presented themselves that allowed me to sell this one business and move on to another (and another), starting the same cycle all over.

CHAPTER 15

Marketing: Setting Up the Almighty Sale

Looking good is better than feeling good, and you look mahvelous.
Billy Crystal as Fernando

The goals of marketing are simple: get known and "believed," be seen in the right places with the right people and/or at the right events, make a splash worthy of being talked about, build and maintain a "stand-apart" identity, become recognizable by name and reputation, establish credibility (with or without credentials), and keep thrusting your name in front of clients, potential clients and the marketplace in general. (Lots encapsulated in this epistle, so please read this all once again.)

Three Components of Marketing

1. The **brand** is how your business is perceived, its image, and what emotional reaction it elicits. It represents a consistent image that makes up the company and its values. Nike, for example, has brand-positioned itself as not only a designer and supplier of sporting goods, clothing and athletic equipment, but also as a company that makes you feel better about yourself.

2. The **identity** represents the visual aspects that form the brand. This is the readily identifiable image that represents who you are and what you do. This identity needs to come through in everything the company produces, from websites and social media right down to packaging. Nike's "Just Do It" emboldens and invites you to get on

board. There is never anything from Nike that does not convey this message that identifies their brand.

3. The **logo** identifies a business in its most simple form: the Nike Swoosh, Apple's apple with a bite out, The Starbucks siren/mermaid, The MacDonald's golden M arches, and so on. What a logo means is more important than what it looks like. The logo is the highly recognizable component of a company's identity.

Branding Is More Than a Logo

Your brand is what people say about you when you're not in the room.
Jeff Bezos

Many entrepreneurs assume that branding is the creation of an identifiable corporate logo. That is simplistic to a fault. Creating a memorable story about your products/services or company and building an awareness of your corporate culture are the mainstay objectives of a branding strategy. While that may include a logo, that is only one small part of the business's identity.

- Branding is the "why" of your business.
- The best brands are based on values, integrity, and trust.
- You cannot simply create authenticity. You need to build it into your culture.
- Your brand needs to live in the hearts of your customers. It needs to be ingrained.
- Your brand needs to offer a promise.
- Your logo is your brand identity, and needs to focus its design, colors, and symbols to your specific target audience to make sure it is memorable and recognizable in the marketplace. There is a reason multinationals spend millions in creating one simple logo that works, and test it with focus groups and market trials. One major airline spent $10 million on the artwork for their jets. It needed to "fly their colors."
- A strong brand adds value to your business's worth. People do not do business with the same organizations or visit the same places

over and over again simply because they think the product or service is good. They become loyal to the brand, because they feel good about the brand, and everything associated with it. Brands affect us all, even if we do not realize it. Everyone has favorite brands that they go back to repeatedly.

- A brand is what people think of you and feel about you, not what you say you are. We create them through visual cues, people and attitudes, word of mouth, publicity, advertising, and social media.

A logo is an easily recognizable graphic symbol that identifies a company, a commercial product, or any public or private entity. A brand is the idea or image people have in mind when thinking about you.

The Branding Journal

Marketing Is an Artform

Some believe that marketing is the greatest art form of the modern era. In fact, it is persuasive psychology packaged in effusive imaging and art.

Lex Dunn

- It builds awareness and excitement.
- It motivates the viewer (or reader or listener) to act, repeatedly too.
- It flatters and caresses the viewer's ego, appealing to their self-image.
- It bullies the skeptics.
- It invites the viewer to join a club and become one of "us." Wear our logo.
- It is an effort to generate leads, new customers, and retain existing customers.
- It tells the viewers that they can be faster, leaner, more beautiful, sexier, and, simply, better than they are now and better than their peers.
- It insists everyone can get there, even the unworthy.
- It builds on brand recognition to up-sell, cross-sell, and through-sell.
- It endeavors for "stuff" to be recognized and be remembered.

Marketing deceives the viewer and that deception ranges from the subliminal to the ridiculous. Strangely enough, the latter are often more memorable.

- Dancing with a mop around your already sparkling 5,000-foot kitchen is normal.
- Even the unhealthiest of foods are just fine.
- The mundane is very acceptable.
- Your contribution alone will make a world of difference to a cause, or to save a disappearing species, and you will be a far better person for it.

Advertising is the mouthpiece of business.

James R. Adams

Marketing is simply a tactic to generate sales. That is fine. There is nothing wrong with coveting profits. Of course, marketing is also intended to grow market share, launch new products or services, access new markets or target customers, and other noble aspirations, but the end goal is harvesting money.

Playing the Marketing Game. Here's How

These are the cornerstone activities of the marketing game.

- **Awareness**—Get the market to know about you.
- **Credibility**—Establish that you can do what you promise, that you have the experience and know-how to succeed (even if you haven't done it yet—flexible ethics).
- **Image**—Create and promote an identifiable and distinct character for yourself and your company, whereby the market can recognize you apart from other players.
- **Continuity**—Through a regular series of promotional activities, let the market know that you are here to stay.
- **Visibility**—Continual exposure to the public, via media, participation in groups, involvement in the community, and so on.
- **Networking**—Ongoing effort to establish contacts that, in turn, can generate leads.

- **Staying on Top**—Hype successes, enhance image, and assure awareness of your entity in the marketplace.

The Marketing–Business Promotion–Sales Life Cycle

This process needs to be uber-clear. Far too often I have heard these terms used interchangeably, which is wrong.

Marketing targets the sales effort. It is the creative, driving force that designs the image, creates the publicity, generates awareness in the marketplace, selects the most receptive target markets for your enterprise, determines the most appropriate vehicles for promotion, and monitors the market in order to react quickly with new/modified products or services.

Business Promotion is the implementation of market strategies via establishing contacts, networks, advertising, disseminating information, seeking publicity, networking in select circles, creating a splash, and, most importantly, generating leads for potential sales. That is the bottom-line objective of business promotion.

Sales is bringing business and money through the door. Now you can cash your paycheck.

A Doable, Realizable Marketing Plan

The Marketing Plan establishes the steps you would follow to carry out identified marketing strategies designed to deliver the predicted results you are seeking. Here are the key components of a Marketing Plan.

- **The Situation**: What is going on? Where is there an issue or opportunity?
- **The Market Goals**: What exactly do we need to try to accomplish?
- **The Market Strategy**: How can we get there from here?
- **The Budget**: What will it cost?
- **The Timelines**: How long will it take?
- **The Milestones**: What can we expect along the way?
- **The Monitoring**: How are we doing? What are we accomplishing? Can we measure the results?
- **The Follow Through**: Is it working? If not, how do we adjust it?

The objective is to generate a Marketing Plan that is workable and realizable. It also needs to be a Plan that an outside party, such as an investor, can readily 'buy into'. If the Plan is too overpowering or complex, it will end up being a bookend on your shelf. A costly one, too. So let's look at what makes a Marketing Plan right for you.

- **Delivery**: Set your expectations as to what marketing will do for you. Sales? New clients? Market share? Social media buzz? Branding? Be specific where you can, that is, xx new clients.
- **Affordability**: Identify activities that your business can afford. It makes no sense creating an advertising campaign that will dwindle your cash flow. The Plan needs to focus on what is effective but doable within a budget.
- **Timing**: Determine how long each campaign or activity will last.
- **Value Proposition**: Was it worth it? Monitor the results in terms of quantifiable outcomes.
- **Adjust or Repeat**: Determine the next implementation phase of the Marketing Plan.

And one more piece of advice worth reiterating here. **Never stop marketing**. It generates the lifeblood of the business, namely sales and cash. Businesses caught in a downward spin or with a cash flow crunch tend to cut their marketing costs. This is so very wrong. They should be increasing their marketing to generate activity.

You Are Your Company's Biggest Marketing Asset

If you are your company's CEO, you are its voice, its vision, and its public face. You have to be able to enter a business meeting, a social gathering, a networking event, and one-on-one interviews, and be able to command attention and inspire confidence.

It has been widely researched and proven that if people like you, respect you, and are inspired by you, they will bestow these same feelings on your company. The importance of this cannot be overstated. You are your company. Your audience must trust that you know every aspect of your business.

Do You Realize That You Are the "Brand Champion"?

The various media are key in bringing your brand to the marketplace, but as important as printed, videoed, online, and social media are, there is no substitution for face-to-face, person-to-person communication. They are called **Brand Champions**, your spokespeople, and they are an absolute necessity in promoting and maintaining your brand. It is like a neighbor who just bought a new mower and cannot stop telling you about it. You have to do the same for your business community. The Brand Champion can be you, or someone whom you consistently delegate to be the "front person."

> *The speed of the leader determines the speed of the gang.*
>
> Mary Kay Ash

Guerilla Marketing: Big Impact for Small Dollars

The true philosophy to follow is, "Go creative or go home." That is the essence of Guerilla Marketing—making a big impression with big ideas, not big budgets.

Guerilla marketing is looking at a small budget and trying to squeeze every penny's worth from it. It means original, creative thinking. It goes beyond "thinking outside the box." It means that *you* design "the box." Sometimes it means there is no box.

Make it experiential. For example, if you are a food-based business, then get your food in front of people: in city squares, inside malls, in parking lots, or even in partnership with others that offer something complimentary to your products/services.

Make it impossible to ignore. Events that encourage audience participation are popular and highly effective, but sometimes, you can simply entertain an audience to get their attention.

The Amazing Impact of Guerilla Marketing

There are some great examples of successful guerilla marketing, including the website that exhibits "100 Best Guerilla Marketing Campaigns."

Definitely worth a visit, and a place to get some ideas, too. Check out https://anerdsworld.com/best-100-guerilla-marketing-campaigns.

It's the unexpected. People are accustomed to seeing advertising on billboards, in magazines, on TV, online, and any and all other traditional venues. This makes it hard to stand out because people are good at "blending" familiar things together to create a seamless background. That's just the way the brain works.

But when you put things in places or situations where they don't "belong," our brain notices it right away because our brains are trying to incorporate the image or event into familiar patterns. They stand out and they get noticed.

Guerilla marketing can be a very affordable and effective way to get your message out. Humor and fun are key elements of guerilla marketing.

You just have to trust your madness.

Clive Barker

Sweet Jesus Ice Cream: A Guerrilla Marketing Winner

Here's one of my favorites: Sweet Jesus Ice Cream (www .sweetjesusicecream.com). The company makes handcrafted ice cream. They named themselves Sweet Jesus because they expect everyone to exclaim those words after they taste their "pimped-out" (no joke) treats. They built a huge following and, in the process, offended a few people. But they got attention too. They now have branches across North America (United States, Canada) and are franchising. This is an example of "guerilla marketing," which is often brazen and exploitive, sometimes politically incorrect, but usually highly effective.

Hilarious Examples of Guerilla Marketing Gone Bad

For promotion purposes for the film, "Mission: Impossible III," digital devices were placed in thousands of newspaper vending boxes in Los Angeles. They played the movie's theme tune aloud whenever the door was opened. The public mistook the devices for bombs and several newsstands were detonated by the bomb squad. An LA hospital was even evacuated

for 90 minutes when the perceived threat was reported (https://www.bbc
.com/news/entertainment-arts-51627622, BBC News Entertainment &
Arts, February 26, 2020).

The promotion for the movie "Devil Baby Attack" featured a mon-
strous baby in a stroller. The doll popped up and screamed at passersby
in the street. It terrified the public, but, on the positive side, this low
budget film received tons of media attention on virtually every TV
network—("Latest Horror-Movie Ad Prank, with a Screaming Devil
Baby, Is Completely Messed Up." *Adweek,* January 14, 2014). It's like the
old Hollywood cliche "I don't care what you say about me, as long as you
keep talking about me."

Snapple Popsicles set up a 25-foot popsicle comprised of 17.5 tons of
flavored, colored ice. Unfortunately, the stunt was set up in New York's
Times Square on an 80-degree June summer day. The firefighters had to
be called in to deal with the kiwi–strawberry flood.

Las Vegas's famous Heart Attack Grill offers massive "Bypass" burgers
and "Flatliner" fries and buttermilk shakes. This guerilla marketing promotion was cute until a diner suffered a heart attack eating their "Triple
Bypass" burger.

There are lessons to be learned here.

Mission Statements Are Simply Public Relations Marketing Fluff

Don't believe your own PR-generated Mission Statement. All those glowing corporate Mission Statements are drafted by marketing people and
intended to demonstrate to customers that the companies are "good corporate citizens."

While save the California condor, clean the environment, and lower
carbon footprints are all admirable, they are simply window dressing
when you consider that the only mission of any company is to maximize
returns to shareholders. Period.

Recommunication: Leave Something to the Imagination

Leave something on the table when you pitch. You always need to have
something to give up, for example, price, perks, something you are

prepared to part with. This allows the customer to claim a "win" while you have only lost something you were prepared to surrender.

Also, in any proposal. Try to leave something to the imagination of the reader. In that way, it will encourage questions and inquiries. Encouraging communication is an important objective of all marketing and promotion packages.

Competition: Ever-present, Insidious, and Yes, Beatable

You have your own business with its own planned direction, standards of performance, and projected goals and objectives. Don't get distracted from your game plan. That also doesn't mean operating in a vacuum either. You have to remain aware of what is going on around you because, depending on the nature of your enterprise, you will be forced to react to market changes, and that may include changes instituted by your competition.

Even in a Shangri-la environment, your very existence and success will generate competition, either from new people on the scene or from existing companies who will expand their scope to encompass what you are doing. It's inevitable. (Incidentally, I have been to Shangri-La, China, and it's quite a disappointment. No temples hanging in the clouds. No enchanting music in the background. Just a couple of souvenir shops and a dusty grocery store. Kind of shabby, actually. Reality sucks sometimes.)

However, the more unique you are, the more of a pioneer and a "renegade" you are, the greater the likelihood that you will be setting industry and market standards that others will aspire to. Once you are in the forefront, with an established reputation and image, and with a solid base for growth, the less you have to fret over "also-rans" in hot pursuit.

But, no matter what field of endeavor you are involved in, or simply entertaining, never become complacent about competition. They are out there, or soon will be. They are devious, jealous, territorial, and ruthless. If you succumb to pressures and temptations and play the game within their rules, you'll be spinning your tires instead on concentrating on business.

If you can take everything they throw at you and, where necessary, adjust your game plan to compensate, you will come out the winner.

Don't worry about competition. Make them worry about you.

This Is How It Works in Real Life

After I had been in business for several years and had succeeded in building a fairly decent clientele, the reputation of our organization was becoming well established in the business community. Although our consulting services were fairly unique, there was competition from various independent consulting groups as well as from professional accounting firms.

None of this competition bothered me. I knew what we could do for the client. The business continued to flourish, regardless of competitors' sniping, to which I remained outwardly oblivious. Inwardly, I remained constantly on guard and wary of competitors infringing on my "turf," or promoting themselves in my style, copycatting my approach.

One day, out of absolutely nowhere, one of my young consultants came to me with a personal dilemma. A competitor, who was in existence before us, but who had been left in a trail of dust from our rapid growth and success, offered this consultant a very lucrative position, meaning double the salary, a fancy title, perks, and so on. The only condition of his employment was that he bring with him our firms' complete client and contacts list, along with other internal documents. Our people always displayed incredible loyalty, mostly because they were treated extremely fairly, and strong personal ties were well entrenched in the working relationship, so the dilemma was really how to get these guys off his back. He remained loyal to my company and became one of my trusted team leaders.

That is what you can expect from competition—the unexpected. And the biggest mistake you can make is to waste your time being paranoid about their next move, or deliberately trying to sabotage or undermine their efforts.

Successful businessmen share the ability to hire people smarter than they are.

Dillard Munford

Build loyalty with your people. Buy it (or rent it, since even allegiance can be temporary) with appreciation (gifts, bonuses, holidays, or "ego-perks" such as reserved parking spots, impressive titles or a bigger office). It will save you from the need to constantly listen for footsteps behind you.

The same goes for clients. Good, repeat clients own your business. Make sure they know you recognize their value.

CHAPTER 16

Sales Are Your Lifeblood

Everyone has an invisible sign hanging from their neck saying 'Make me feel important'.

Mary Kay Ash

The Lifeblood of a business is working capital, which is generated by sales. Sales means closing the deal, securing the purchase order, or moving the merchandise. It represents generating revenues for your business. (Can you just hear Tom Cruise, as Jerry Maguire, the sports agent, yelling into his phone "Show me the money!".)

Selling is the harsh reality of one-on-one "confrontations" with would-be clients. If you cannot reach your audience on a one-to-one basis, you will fail miserably. They (the bank, who else?) may even repossess your Porsche.

This Handbook has discussed marketing, hot buttons that initiate customer action, the psychology of business, skating, bluffing, and various other rarely disclosed secrets of doing business. However, the final episode is generating sales. **No sales = no working capital = no business.**

Your Marketplace Is a Pie

Your market may be finite, or slow to grow. Barring tech toys and dazzling advancements, most markets grow (or shrink) in bits and increments. So think of your marketplace as a pie of limited size. Only so many slices to go around. How much of the pie do you want to steal? Who are you going to "steal" it from? Yes, I said "steal," because your competitors have all carved out their share, leaving few crumbs for newbies. You will be plundering the pie for your piece.

With this image in mind, you need to assume that others out there are watching you, nervous about you, jealous of you, and, with the slightest provocation, will be vindictive toward you. Forewarned is being prepared to do battle.

Sales at Virtually Any Cost

Every dollar you spend should be directly linked with activities and expenses that generate revenues. This applies to start-ups, second-stage companies, or those in full throttle. Creating wealth is a business's number 1 priority. Make it yours too, and drill it into your team as well. Cash is king. Buying your new Porsche can wait. Think sales, sales, sales.

The Dance Is Over. Ask for Business

After you and your client have done the dance, don't hesitate to ask for their business. Too many businesspeople leave sales calls as open-ended. Wrong. Ask for the order. The client's time is valuable, as is yours, and the dance can only go on for a while. When the music stops, ask for the business. It is not off-putting to be bold. Go ahead.

Subtle (and Some Less-Subtle) Sales-Closing Techniques

- **Be noble**. It's a Jekyll and Hide thing. Start with flattery to win over the customer, then play the devil's advocate, for example, "Your website is pretty great, but I can make it more effective and draw more traffic."
- **Empathize** with the client, regardless what is being discussed, such as "Bad day? You can't believe what I went through last Tuesday. Sounds just like that. I know, I know." Try delivering this sincerely. Whether it's true or not does not matter.
- **Agree** with just about everything, disregarding what you may not actually agree with. An ally becomes a trusted bunkie.
- **Flattery and egocentric appeal**. People are ego-hounds and like being complimented. So exalt them effusively about their business,

reputation, brand, the picture of their family on their desk, you name it. Get them on side.

- **Join their club** by possibly stating "I'm just like that too." Clubbies support each other.
- **The groveling**. This is a time-honored classic, but needs a subtle touch. Try "I know you're busy, so I'll be back tomorrow, ok?" That is fine. But avoid the kitschy, like "This is the last sale unit, then the price goes up 20 percent." That's just tasteless.
- **Little white lies**. This is a core doctrine of flexible ethics. Make stuff up, but not in a damaging way. You might try "My team can handle that" (my team being me).
- **Ask questions** you already know the answers to.
- **Tell business stories**. People love stories with happy endings.
- **Appeal to emotion**. People tend to decide partly or wholly emotionally. Sell from the heart. Show compassion (real or otherwise). Practice.
- **Be persuasively gentle**. Customers don't like to be sold. But they do love to buy. Think about that one.
- **Consensus.** People follow crowds, sometimes almost sheeplike. If others have dealt with you, or bought your products or services, that implies others have already done the research and have made the current customer's decision easier for them. It's an instant comfort level for the customer.

Always go into a meeting with a clear definition of what outcome you want, such as securing a follow up meeting, or being asked for a proposal or a sales commitment. Let your target set your actions.

Courteous treatment will make a customer a walking advertisement.

J. Graham

Use Human Nature in Generating Sales

Human nature is the imprinted behavior that people exhibit. Few areas of business are as impacted by human nature as sales. According to (a loosely paraphrased excerpt from) *Entrepreneur Magazine* (Ted Chong, October 2018), these are the key ingredients of human nature that salespeople need to be aware of, and, consequently, learn to manipulate.

- **People avoid pain more than gaining pleasure**. The implication here is to appeal to prospective customers' business pains and help them seek pain relief. Identify what the pain points are and sell to alleviate them. Be the hero.
- **Humans are naturally inquisitive**. There is a need to fill any gap between what we know and what we need or want to know. So, fill the gap.
- **We all have a deep-seated interest in ourselves**. We are number 1. So, appeal to that egocentric drive. Flatter them, and their business. Make them look good to others. Feed that self-interest. Be their fan club, their groupie.
- **People stubbornly believe what they want to believe**. So don't tell them they are wrong. That challenges their beliefs. Instead, tell them you believe too. (That sounds like a perfect example of 'flexible ethics', right?)
- **Instant gratification rules**. We are a lazy species. You need to focus on showing early results of some kind (with more that can then follow downstream).
- **Quick is good** as it would justify their decision to go with you. Fast, quantifiable results.

Sales Trash Talk

There are a number of overused, mostly old-time sales techniques that just can't seem to go away. We tend to associate these with bright polyester suits and mismatched ties of car salesmen, but, in fact, like a bad meal, they seem to hang around, tired, and unwelcomed. Try to avoid these.

- **Now or never** — "This is the last one" or "The sale is over tonight."
- **Painting into a corner** — "Can you make this decision on your own?"
- **Let's go** — "Is there a reason we can't start today?"
- **Assumptive close**, before there is an agreed-upon sales — "We can deliver this Tuesday, will that be okay?"
- **Mean-mouthing competition**. That is always a turn off. As mentioned before, you cannot build your business on your competitor's back.

Avoid Confrontations

Business is often seen as a series of wins and losses, and that includes trying to generate sales. It's perceived as black and white. But while getting to the win/lose, there are inevitably a series of skirmishes, standoffs, confrontations, and impactful dialogue.

Pick your battles. The successful businessperson learns to recognize that tactful concessions and accommodations in the selling process allow you to stand firm on key matters when it counts, and when to back away to keep the dialogue open.

Focus on the substantive and let others own the petty stuff.

Think sales. That's the prize.

Dress to Mirror Your Clients

As a business consultant, I chose my meeting clothes carefully, always making sure to reflect my clients' comfort levels. Sometimes it was a sports shirt and rolled up sleeves, other times it was my Armani threads. I also had two vehicles, a clunker and a beast. If I knew the client would admonish my spend-free attitude and think my fees were too high because I was driving the beast, I would make sure to arrive in my older car. If my client wanted to engage me because if I was successful then they would be successful hiring me, I dressed (and drove) for success. It worked. Seems silly, but business is a game, remember?

So never overwhelm your client or potential client with your bling and $4,500 suit unless, of course, they are also swanky exhibitionists.

Be Nice to Brain-Dead People

Years ago I was called upon to help turn around a long-standing business that was caught competing against an onslaught of cheap Asian imports. At a crucial strategic planning session, the owner's son got up and said he had a solution. "We need to lower our costs and raise our selling prices," the simpleton said. Silence ensued. I thanked him for his valuable insight and carried on with more constructive planning. I was (painfully) nice to him as he was the aging owner's pending successor. Sometimes dignity is in short supply in business.

An "Elevator Pitch" Can Win Business for You

An elevator pitch (or a "sales pitch") is an overview of who you are, what you do, and how you can help the listener. It is you selling yourself in a brief and concise manner. In reality, an elevator pitch is a quick and effective opening salvo anytime you have an opportunity to promote your business.

The perfect pitch should be no longer than 45 seconds, which is about 200 words. So imagine you are getting into the elevator at street level, deliver your pitch to a client or investor before you both get off at the eighth floor. It starts with an "attention-getting" hook to capture the listener's attention. This could be a question or a statement that really entices them to listen to you for the full 45 seconds.

You will use your elevator pitch every time you meet anyone whom you want to impress, sell to or inaugurate into your contacts network. The hook is also critical when you are at a networking function and the person you have just met is already looking over your shoulder for the next meet up. Seize their full attention with a powerful hook. Here are a couple of movie script hooks, and you will see why these open up dialogue with whomever they were trying to impress.

- "Imagine twins separated at birth and they are reunited as grown men. One is Danny DeVito and the other is Arnold Schwarzenegger." (Writer's pitch for the movie "Twins")
- "The serial killer wasn't on trial. He was on the jury." (This was the irresistible pitch on a book cover.)

A business elevator pitch can be broken down into four components, all of which come together in one fluid delivery, in rapid succession, and within a short time frame. Remember that people's attention spans are almost childlike, especially with the onslaught on the Internet and the web's ability to retain your attention for only about 8 seconds per webpage visit (that's a fact), so be succinct in your rendition.

1. **The "hook"** grabs their attention, like "My clients increase their web traffic by 59 percent."

2. **The "What's in it for me" (WIIFM)** focuses on the benefits to the listener, for example, "That means more profit for you, and more time for you to focus on other parts of your business."

3. **The "credibility,"** which might be something like "I am good at this and have been at this for 20 years. I deliver for my clients. You can talk to them, if you like."

4. **The "call to action,"** being very proactive, such as "Let's book some time next week and we can talk more and get specific."

You have to use simple language in your pitch. This is not a case of dumbing it down, rather ensuring that anyone can understand it whether they are in your industry or not. If you use too much jargon, you tend to alienate most laymen and their minds start to wander as a result. Be witty or just very different—the point is that a pitch will only be memorable if it stands out.

At the end of the pitch, you will want the listener to think, "how can we do business?"

Customer Service Should Be Your Religion

Your most unhappy customers are your greatest source of learning.
                                                                    Bill Gates

The rule of thumb is that it takes 10 times as much effort and cost to attract a new customer than keeping an existing customer happy. Repeat customers represent 20 percent of your customers, yet they account for 80 percent of your business. What does that tell you? Yet, businesses are constantly chasing down new clients, generally at the expense of absolutely treasuring and coddling existing customers.

Customer service means providing service to customers before, during, and after a purchase. It is nonstop and doesn't end with a sale. It requires patience and tolerance (especially with finicky and painful customers), attentiveness, great communications skills, and even acting ability. Learn to perform. You and your people need to hone these theatrics. Be genuinely (or, failing that, disingenuously) nice. Hire an acting coach if you need to. Yes, I have mentioned this before, and I am doing so again. It is important. Seriously. The benefits are huge.

Ever get a gift that the retailer hassled you about when you tried to return it? Ever shop there again? There you go.

Pre-research before an Important Sales Meeting

If there is a lot at stake at an upcoming meeting, do your homework before the get-together. Find out everything you can from websites, social media, annual reports, trade magazine articles, association data, and other sources. It will impress the would-be client and provide you with a fair amount of insight and ammunition for your meeting.

Feel free to drop tidbits of information at the meeting. The client will be flattered that you have taken the time to educate yourself. Flattery works. It is a motivation-to-act trigger, remember?

This Is How It Works in Real Life

My company was hired to carry out third-party research on behalf of a Fortune 500 firm, which was interested in creating a line of "green," environmentally friendly baby diapers. The goal was to use processed peat moss as the absorbent. They were quite keen on this project. Their marketing people were already salivating at the prospects.

Our mandate was to examine the sources of enough quality-grade peat moss to fill their needs. They had identified Russia as their top raw materials supply chain.

Knowing all of this in advance, we put our best researchers to work. At our first planning meeting with all of their team present, we ever so gently informed them that their primary Russian raw materials source was far too close to Chernobyl, and the peat moss would be contaminated for roughly another 100 years.

They were horrified. Imagine, diapers filled with radioactive peat moss! The marketing team envisioned babies glowing at night. The lawyers were already imagining pending class action suits (and likely overjoyed at the prospect). The entire project was scrapped.

We had saved the company from imminent danger and untold liability, and they rewarded us with significant additional consulting work for years to come.

You cannot make up stories like this.

So, prescreen pending meetings with clients and find out as much as you can before you walk through the door. It will serve you well.

CHAPTER 17

Be Yourself, or Someone Else: Playacting Is Part of Business

Don't confuse my personality with my attitude. My personality is who I am. My attitude depends on who I am with.

Frank Ocean

In everyday life, we automatically assume different roles. We bluster when the occasion calls for bragging rights. We cower when we are menaced and we intimidate when we throw temper tantrums or squeal to get our way. We anger when we become indignant and skulk when we are caught.

Playacting or roleplaying is almost a mechanical act in response to a situation that calls for a reaction to a stimulus. It is a pretense, a deception, a ruse, an act. And we do it every day.

In any networking situation or where you are in a situation where you are "on stage," such as selling a product/service, or promoting yourself at a trade show or conference, you may need to take on the role of the businessperson you want others to see. In business it is often a learned response. Never let anyone see anything but that. Never let your guard down.

This is called "playacting". Stay in character. Your anxiety will be reduced by roleplaying. So put on your phony face!

Take Acting Classes for Business Impact

Actors use drama to make their performance memorable. For the business person, drama translates to communicating business impact.

Richard Fouts

As a businessperson, you are an entertainer. Every situation (meeting, networking, presentation) should inspire an action from your audience. Whatever you say, whatever you do, all add to your role as the businessperson. Taking a few seconds to respond builds anticipation. Body language gives the audience clues as to who you are and what you want.

Acting classes give you that other "creative self" in you to draw on. The entertainer. Acting techniques expand your selling and communications repertoire. Here are a number of important business acting lessons.

- There are two main types of actors: character and persona. Character actors become someone else. Think Johnny Depp, Meryl Streep, or Daniel Day Lewis. Persona actors apply their own personalities into a role, like Harrison Ford, Jennifer Aniston, and Tommy Lee Jones. Regardless of their role, you always recognize them in the roles they take on.
- Decide which type of actor you can be. Whichever acting path you follow, it needs to be sustainable, repeatable, and believable.
- Your attire is your "costume." It needs to match the situation (meeting, presentation, etc.) and your own persona. In fact, your outfit needs to project your persona. So have a variety of looks that project aspects of your persona.
- Actors warm up. That means stretching to be limber, including limbering up your voice, mouth, and speech. It may sound odd, but this enhances your performance.
- Work on your smile, real or forced.
- Check yourself before you enter the "stage"; outfit, posture (and even makeup).
- Enter with a purpose.
- Take a moment to assess the situation, the people you are meeting, or hoping to meet, and the surroundings. Don't leap into action.

- Choose your words carefully. These are called "operative words" and are the ones the listeners need to hear to stay involved in your performance.
- In an encounter, maintain eye contact, listen, and pay attention to what is going on and be aware of the "power of proximity." Being reasonably close is okay.
- Towering over somebody or uncomfortable "in-your-face" proximity is exceedingly awkward. It will shorten your "together time'" dramatically. It is the "off switch" for receptivity.
- Hold your audience. Ask questions. Keep the dialogue going. Keep up your energy. But also, short "pregnant pauses" show calmness and confidence. Balance it all out.
- Your performance tactics need to be able to initiate action. How do you do that? Build an arsenal of delivery maneuvers. Your speech and accompanying body language can be flattering, empathetic, entertaining, or any nuance that will solicit a positive response. That's called acting.
- Above all, enjoy the performance. It will show.

Become a Chameleon: The Business Actor

I always wanted to be somebody, but now I realize I should have been more specific.

Lily Tomlin

- When you act out a business role, make sure it is one that you are capable of performing.
- Many people enjoy hiding behind a mask in the course of their encounters. It gives them a new arena and freedom of expression, and bolsters their confidence. After all, if they are not liked by someone, it's directed toward their alter ego and not really at them, and they do not take any personal offense in any setback.
- Different businesses demand different personalities. In fact, business people look for stereotypes with the people they deal with.
- People, in general, are very comfortable when they know what they are dealing with, when they can apply a label to you. They select

their entire response mode to dealing with you by virtue of what they expect from someone in your profession. This is entirely to your advantage.

- Business people like pseudo renegades, but they don't tolerate weirdos. The former get the job done in their own distinct style, while the latter are undependable and fail—that's the illusion of imaging.
- Match your interests with an appropriate persona, and study the other players out there.
- Steadfastly cling to your predetermined image, for you and your organization.
- As you gain experience, your exposure and confidence grows. Experiment and deviate somewhat from the image by developing a style and approach that makes you distinctly individual, markedly different and therefore, in the eyes of your would-be clients and industry contacts, unquestionably better. You become the successful renegade.
- In this entire process of roleplaying, if there is a wide discrepancy between who you really are and who you have to be in your business environment, maintain a veritable stranglehold on reality.
- Don't start to believe your own hype, and for goodness sake, steadfastly maintain that "spectator mode" so that your business ego does not slip gently and without warning into your true identity.
- In playacting, "right and wrong" are very vague frameworks of flexible ethics and only you can decide what is acceptable to you.

It's Not Who You Are, It's Who You Need to Be

If this presents a challenge for you, then courses in motivational speaking or communications would help. As well, you should attend as many networking sessions as you can to hone your skills. But go to events where they do not know you. It's a tougher crowd, and if you mess up, well, who cares?

Another good tip is to attend trade shows and conferences, and study how others represent themselves and their companies. Remember that, in the eyes of people you meet, you are your company. They will judge your business based on the impression they get in meeting you, or dealing with you.

Think of it as being "on," continuously, in every face-to-face meeting, business gathering, business lunch, and even your e-mails, blogs, social media and other avenues of communicating and correspondence. You need to be consistent in the message you are delivering.

This Is How It Works in Real Life

In one of my businesses, it was critical that I connect with upper management of prospective clients, including the board, and highly placed government people. This was no easy task. I was regularly stonewalled by an executive assistant whose job was to screen out possible "irritants" such as me. However, without connecting, I was stifled.

One day, out of total frustration, I asked my own executive assistant to try, thinking that her rapport with those blocking my access would be better than mine. It certainly couldn't be any worse!

I should explain that she was pretty timid, and tended to stumble and stutter somewhat when under pressure. She quickly set her sights on the guardians of the palace. Her charming country-bumpkin persona including delivering lines like "You have to help me, please. My boss will be very upset if I can't get him an appointment with your boss." She related to them amazingly well. I was never sure if this was really her, or an act she had developed. Regardless, it worked.

I kind of think it was an act though, because even after years of running interference for me on booking those meetings, she still delivered that "help me I am vulnerable" act. Now, she was a performer!

CHAPTER 18

Running Your Business, Not Vice Versa

Hope is not a strategy.

Joel Book

When you were young, your mother likely said to you "Eat everything on your plate. You took it. You eat it." Or, perhaps you just heard my mother say it to me. She had a booming voice that carried.

Business is no different. You have built a business. You sacrificed, sweated, worried, and finally succeeded in building something worthwhile. It's your baby. Now you need to deal with its need for constant attention, its crying jags, and yes, even its soiled diapers. You know, the fun stuff.

Business demands your attention. It insists on it, or it will feel unloved and throw a tantrum or two. It has your DNA. It cannot exist without your presence. The details. The day-to-day repetition. The competition couched in pettiness. The people. The employees. That's right, the boring, mundane stuff.

Managing Your Business Risk

Managing risk for an existing business is far different than risk assessment for opportunities. You are not examining a shiny coin of an opportunity. Instead, you are addressing and weighing problems, and determining the least damaging course of action to pursue. Risk assessment for an operating business is more like damage control, such as when a competitor is infringing on your market, or your technology, or when you are hiring additional staff or running a marketing campaign that might dangerously stretch your cash flow. You need to weigh the consequences and choose.

"Putting out fires" and short-term "Band-Aid solutions" are sometimes inevitable, but are not long-term coping strategies, and certainly not consistent with your need to effectively run a business.

Operational Risk

"Operational Risk Management" is the process of identifying possible risks, problems, or even disasters before they happen, setting up procedures to avoid the risk, and adopting strategies to minimize risk, or at the very least help cope with its impact.

- Your team/management meetings should include a frank discussion on what challenges may be on the horizon across every aspect of the business. This should include not only red-flagging but putting the mitigating strategies in place to deal with them, and allocating sufficient resources to do so effectively.
- Design policies to prevent identifiable risks and conflicts. One such example is setting credit policy guidelines and the awarding of credit limits to customers.

The Lesser of Two Evils

The truth is that many of the operational risks you might face are unexpected and pressing. They arrive out of left field and stare you down. Your business experience and ability to calmly gage the implications of the alternative solutions are your greatest weapons. Where there is no real solution, then your course of action is the one that is the least disruptive to your business. The lesser of evils.

Business Pain Points. Stop Whining

Welcome to your first world problems. Enjoy the variety of business pain points that will be yours and yours alone to deal with. What are business pain points? What customers and/or staff complain about. Legitimate beefs? Sometimes. Petty? Possibly. Need to be prioritized? Definitely. Need to be addressed? Selectively.

"We don't have enough money." "Our website sucks." "Our business partner is a jerk." "The employees are coasting." "Competitors are better at advertising." They range from the absurdly petty ("I haven't taken a vacation in a month") to the personal ("This business is like a jail sentence") and to the serious and very injurious ("Customer complaints are up 35 percent").

I can accept failure. Everyone fails at something. But I cannot accept not trying.

Michael Jordan

Business pain points may be internal, or related to your customers. The list is endless. These business pain points may be valid, but nobody should care about these bellyaches except you:

- Don't let them fester. The key is finding solutions quickly.
- Don't initiate any whining, and certainly don't accept any from your people.
- Avoid making assumptions. Get to the source of the issue. First-hand sources only.
- Listen to whomever has brought the pain point forward. That can be staff, customers, suppliers, business friends, or associates. Then ask them for their ideas to resolve the issues.
- Work to determine if these pain points are real or fabricated. If they are fabricated, then why? Consider the source and the reasoning for their action.
- Dissect and peel back all the issues around the pain point. It may not be as serious as its outward appearance has led you to believe.
- Find any commonality. Business pain points rarely live a solitary life.
- Don't use them as an excuse for not delivering for your customers. Most important of all, just deal with them.

Employees Are Just Employees

Surrounded by good people with team spirit and dedication, you can accomplish anything. However, surrounded by strutting prima donnas whose first interest is their own, and where catfights are the office entertainment, you will have serious issues.

Your staff reflects your mood, and they react to your management style.

- If you are tyrannical, they will cower and do whatever to cover their tracks. If there are any problems, you will likely find out only after considerable damage has been done.
- If you are everybody's best friend, you will get walked on and trampled. Your ability to manage, set company policies, and even discipline will be minimalized.
- Don't open a confessional and listen to everybody's transgressions and foibles.

Striking a compromise in a workable business environment is key. The office setting is not a confessional, nor is it a holy doctrine of heavenly behavior. Stuff happens. People make personal mistakes that find their way into the office. Determine what will simply go away on its own, and what needs direct intervention because it has consequences on your business. You be the judge.

Make Technology Your Friend

This section is not a dissertation on social media, web design, and being number 1 on the Google search engine. There are untold "how-to" books, websites, videos, webinars, and geeks out there to help you.

Technology can work for you, but be selective. E-mail blast programs, web development templates, sales platforms, and so on, are all great tools. But social media is so overcrowded it can also become a graveyard. A huge time drain too.

I joined Facebook and now have friends I would never, ever consider associating with, and I know too much about their relationships and their favorite coffee bars too. I quit Facebook as fast as I could.

I joined LinkedIn, posted great blogs (got multiple "likes") and watched as a post of Fall fashion faux purses got thousands of hits. And now, most of the drivel on there is people trying to sell me stuff. They come on like my long lost friends, which is annoying and assumptive. I quit LinkedIn too.

So, yes, technology and all its inbred cousins are great, but be selective. Or find someone skilled to handle it all for you, and just get back to running your business.

Reward the Ones Who Got You There

I have always been a firm believer in rewards as a motivator. It is not just the reward itself, but the positive impact of recognition and approval. People like to be reminded of how important they are to you and your organization.

I have had my share of being belittled by "bosses" in my early corporate years (pre-entrepreneurship). They were petty. They were abusive and uncaring. They de-inspired me. And I swore I would never replicate their management style. I never did.

You can use psychological rewards, for example, "employee of the month," or physical rewards, such as bonuses, vacations, or whatever carrots work. But don't forget that these are the people who have helped you succeed. They deserve to know it.

Who Can Help You Plan, Grow, and Succeed

I came from an environment where if you see a snake, you kill it. At General Motors, if you see a snake, the first thing you do is hire a consultant on snakes.

H. Ross Perot

Consultants can be useful if you make sure that (a) they understand what you need, and (b) they don't see you as a meal ticket to get their family to the Caribbean for 4 weeks, and (c) most importantly, you are dealing with a consultant who has had hands-on entrepreneurial background. Here is what my experience has shown me:

Academics are okay as long as they have direct business experience. Former government people are out. I have found their work ethically lacking.

Accountants deal with history and have minimal forward-looking skills, so they are also out.

Lawyers are out because they often do not know nearly as much as they claim to.

Finally, get someone who won't just regurgitate everything you tell them and then call it original thoughts.

This Is How It Works in Real Life

For a while in my corporate career, I was Group Controller for 26 different companies under the umbrella of an investment fund. My role included assessing opportunities as well as troubleshooting where there were serious problems.

One of the businesses under my charge was a manufacturer of office furniture. The plant was on strike, and had been for 2 months. My job was to suggest the next move on behalf of the fund.

The business was not terribly profitable, and the shutdown was taking its toll on its market share as well. Competitors were bloodying each other in a feeding frenzy. Had I been on the other side of the situation, I would have too.

The plant was unionized, and I mean with a dreadfully militant union. Equipment in the plant was being vandalized, so a lockout was in place. Picket lines were up daily. Delivery vans were being defaced and damaged.

The management, office, and sales staff were demoralized and fearful. That was understandable. However, what was surprising was that the unionized staff was painfully distrustful of the ownership. I offered to show the union's forensic accountant the statements and books of the business, to which they agreed. There was, after all, nothing worth hiding.

Two principal owners came to the plant to present the statements to the union's accountants. Knowing the penchant for flamboyance of the owners, and despite my warnings to the contrary, one arrived in his

Lincoln Continental, the other in a Rolls Royce. They parked close to the employees' entranceway. It was immediately ball game over.

The union did not believe the numbers. We were accused of hiding something. Big surprise. I recommended the facility be shut down permanently, which the fund accepted to do. The damage was irreparable. One month later, the empty plant burned to the ground.

With the best of intentions and planning, there is always stuff that will be out of your control, and, inevitably, despite your best plan to deal with challenges, there are blockheads out there who can and will throw you a curve (really, showing up in a Lincoln and a Rolls Royce to a union meeting? Get serious.). Be prepared for the unexpected.

Once again, you just can't make up stuff like this.

Life tries to teach us who are the good guys, the smart guys, and who are the villains, and sometimes you can judge strictly by the cut of their Armani suits and pimped-out cars.

CHAPTER 19

Money, Money, Money

If you want to know the value of money, go and try to borrow some.
Benjamin Franklin

Money is the cornerstone of business. Everything eventually boils down to bucks, whether it's needing funds to start, using working capital to assure growth, gambling on a "sure" scheme, or investing money to make more money. A good idea, exceptional abilities, or "ground floor information" on deals must always be backed up with the dollars to make opportunities happen.

Finance and Stress: A Tag Team Match

From a personal stress perspective, there are some common sense rules to follow that will protect you, your assets, and your sanity.

- Never risk more than you are prepared to lose or, should things go badly, will put you into a position whereby you cannot recover within a short period of time.
- Always enter into a transaction with the best of intentions, but, at the same time, prepare escape clauses that protect you for the worst case, should it arise.
- The more you are prepared to risk, the more certain you had better be convinced of a "sure thing." That means more homework.
- Avoid selling your body and soul, to investors, bankers, etc., so that, even when you do succeed, you are basically doing so for someone else.

Stress serves as a personal safeguard. It plays the devil's advocate in all your decision making by always flashing a preview of the worst possible results of your actions. Many entrepreneurs desperately need some sort of counterbalance like stress to balance their enthusiasm. In effect, it makes you stop and think about the viability and repercussions of your plans and proposed business gambles. It alerts you when there is incongruence between risk and possible loss of financial security. Stress keeps you prudent without completely eliminating your vital entrepreneurial gamblers' instinct. Stress is a barometer of security. The more you jeopardize your status, the higher the stress meter rises.

Risk-taking causes stress. Risk-taking jeopardizes security, both personal and financial. Insecurity causes stress. Stress affects risk-taking. The key to breaking or avoiding this debilitating, unproductive cycle is by prudent, affordable risk-taking, which minimizes the threat to security. Remember, it's your money, or your liability.

Choose Your Investors Wisely

What drives investors? It's a simple equation: earn me profits, protect my investment, and give me an exit strategy ("PPE"). There are other considerations like long-term potential for the sale of the company or the technology, but the cornerstones are almost always PPE.

Understand that and build it into your business presentation model, and you will significantly increase your chances for securing investment. Just tell people what they want and need to hear, and what will get them to act. So, put on your Gucci kneepads, practice genuflecting, and go get it.

Investors should be more than a bank account. We normally associate investors with money, and that is the logical first priority in seeking out venture capital. However, ask yourself, once the honeymoon is over and the money is spent (well spent or otherwise), what now? Are you tied in with monthly fees to your investors? A no-longer contributing business partner? Shareholder debt? Tons of management reports to justify your existence? The point is, you need to do a profile of the ideal investor insofar as what else besides money that you want them to bring to the table. Customers? Setting up distribution channels? Do they possess other useful areas of expertise? Think about it before you take on investors, and all the "baggage" that comes with them.

Avoid Vulture Capital

We all know what venture capital is, and the impressive array of hoops and conditions that these funds often come with. However, the lowest form of venture capital is aptly called "vulture capital." Why? As part of the funding conditions, there is a "ratchet clause." Simply put, you promised to generate $xxx in revenues or profits. If these promised milestones are not met, the vulture has the right to ratchet another percentage of your company. This can continue until you are filling in a job application at the company you used to own. Sounds crazy, but it exists, so beware.

Partnerships: Don't Get Me Started

It would take volumes to expound on partnerships. That in itself is not a good sign as it implies that I have had some doozies. You would be right. So, here is the cynic's checklist of partnerships.

- Make sure there is a clear understanding of what you each bring to the business. (In my first partnership, I secured all the contracts while my partner made coffee and did the bank deposits.)
- Any partnership agreements should not be drawn up by your partner's lawyer. It reminds me of a clause my first partner's lawyer had in the agreement. It was entitled "In the event of the death of Jay," with no provision for my partner's potential death! Just mine.
- Don't go into partnership with someone whose wealth far exceeds yours. In the event of a divorce, they can out-legal you.
- Don't ever go into business with friends, unless you are prepared to bid that friendship goodbye.

Rent Before You Buy

My final advice is, prior to going into partnership, try living together for a year. See how compatible you are together. Learn more about each other's abilities, personalities, ethics, and business dreams. See if your values align in practice. So, rent before you buy.

Personally, I have had a number of business partners. Few worked for long. Perhaps it was me. I found it better to surround myself with an excellent team of hired help.

How to Survive a Partnership

- Exploit partners' strengths and accept their weaknesses.
- Prepare a concise partnership agreement with the outlook that one day you will divorce. Lay out the separation terms in advance, buy-out options, and so on.
- Share the load. Nothing destroys a partnership as fast as inequality.
- Don't take problems or fallings-out personally.
- Work with a clear division of responsibility.
- If there is any mistrust, end the relationship quickly.
- If you feel a lack of confidence in the other's performance, deal with it openly.
- Everyone goes through difficult personal times. A true partner is supportive and does not leap in to take advantage.
- Each party is accountable for their own actions, or inactions.
- In the case of disagreements, one or the other person usually feels stronger about a situation. Go with it. Pick your battles.
- Partnerships other than 50/50 are notoriously lopsided and difficult to work. That goes for shares, salaries, perks, bonuses, and, of course, workload.
- Understand that, over time, people change. Also, people develop at different speeds and in different directions. An open, working partnership maintains the dialogue and flexibility to compensate for changes.
- Keep business and families apart. There is no need to look for trouble if your wife doesn't get along with your partner, or his wife, or his kids, or his cat.
- Avoid jealousy. If your partner scores a coup, it should be shared, not envied.
- Strive for unanimity on all major decisions that affect the growth and direction of your business. Build that into your partnership agreement.
- A partnership is not a competition, but instead, the synergy of forces that result in one singular force greater than the sum total of the individuals.

- Recognize when the partnership is not working and, if it is beyond repair, initiate divorce proceedings. Keep it amicable, if you can, since there are no real winners in such a situation.
- Remember the cornerstones of a partnership: trust, division of responsibility, accountability, confidence, mutual reliance, and, sometimes most of all, some great escape clauses.

The Partnership Courting and Marriage Life Cycle

Partnerships go through a well-defined marriage-like life pattern. Recognizing the model can, just maybe, prepare the entrepreneur for things to come.

- The **courting ritual,** where each partner fans their peacock feathers and proclaims their love for ever after.
- The **marriage proposal**, namely a Letter of Intent. Oh the joy, the ecstasy!
- The **marriage contract**. Here is where reality hits. You want what concessions?
- The **wedding**. Pure kinetic energy. The partners have a new home together, that is, the business.
- The **honeymoon**, where a new relationship melds in a spirit of love and tenderness. (Okay, wait for it.)
- **Growing apart**. This is inevitable. Things change. People change. Struggles ensue. The business changes. Something has to give. Try to make it work.
- The **divorce**. Now, not all partnerships end in divorce. Many continue on for a veritable lifetime. But, where there is a divorce, it is often as bad or worse than a marital divorce.

This Is How It Works in Real Life

Sometimes it's amazing what we do for money, and what position we place ourselves in.

I secured a contract to supply the New Zealand Marine Research Centre with research vessels they wanted to lease for a number of months.

This was a potentially lucrative deal, but what did I know about research vessels?

I had been to Vladivostok, Russia, and witnessed their fleet sitting idle in port. So I connected with a business associate who worked for an engineering firm that serviced the fleet. Together we negotiated a deal and set the framework with the client. Everyone was most pleased. Then reality hit.

The Russian crew had not been paid in months. The vessel had no fuel and was in need of some spare parts sitting in a warehouse awaiting payment. Oh yes, all payments had to be made in cash, U.S. currency only. This was a shocker, since we were dealing with the Russian navy, for goodness sakes.

I secured the cash funds, neatly piled in a briefcase. I now had yet another partner, the investor. I could not use any banks in Vladivostok for transfers because they were notoriously light fingered and also were not allowed to deal in any currency other than inflation-ridden Russian Ruble.

My investor partner was reasonably supportive. I had worked out a game plan when I negotiated for the funding.

So there I was, in Vladivostok, in late fall, temperatures freezing, driving in the back of a canvas-roofed truck heated with a little wood stove, two burly "assistants" next to me as I clung to the cash-filled briefcase. My life flashed before my eyes, but, eventually, the deal was consummated and all fell into place as planned. Everyone was pleased. I was pleased, and very relieved.

It just goes to show to what extremes the entrepreneur will go to. But business is business, right?

CHAPTER 20

There's a Time to Quit. Here's How

If we want to achieve greatness, stop asking for permission.

Eddie Colla

The time for "what-ifs" and "but I should have ..." is over. You have arrived. By your own personal and business standards, you have succeeded. You have probably fallen a little short of your goals but have exceeded what you really thought that you could achieve. That's okay. That's the way it usually works.

Sell your business, take care of your health, and enjoy the ride, and, for goodness sake, do so while you are still healthy enough to do what you always wanted to do! A rocking chair on the beach is not a pretty sight!

Hire someone to value and sell your business. You may want to do it through a third party, with anonymity, especially if you do not want to disclose your intentions to your staff and clients.

Do What Is Right for You, Just for You

Do whatever is right for you, but do not decide spontaneously. Think about all the alternatives. Instinctively, you may want to get out, since you have achieved your goals, and with the full knowledge that not only was the cost high in getting to where you are, but also continuance along the same path may extract too much, may risk what you have, and may demand more of you than you are prepared to offer.

Creative Burnout

Up to now, your creative and innovative talents have been key elements in your success. Your resources have seemed limitless, easily accessed when called upon. Ideas and concepts were bold and almost effortless.

Suddenly, everything you are coming up with is virtually a rehash of past ideas and approaches. Nothing really new seems to be generating. It takes more concentration to focus. Paranoia and self-doubt set in, coloring your perspective, questioning your judgment. Input from others becomes threatening, and any deviation from the past is instantly branded flawed, risky, and doomed to failure, regardless of merit.

The business will suffer unless you take the opportunity to recharge your batteries, bring in new creative blood, or step aside.

Time to Go?

You will know when it's time to get out. Your focus may wane, or you will become distracted by personal interests. Or, you may feel you have achieved what you set out to do, and there is nothing left to "prove" and it's just time. As that crossroad approaches, choose an exit strategy. Your best bet is to sell your business.

Succession Is Often Impractical

Leaving it to the kids has often proved to be a fatal approach. You have raised them, spoiled them, and have likely not instilled that die-hard entrepreneurial drive that has attributed to your success and longevity at the helm. Empires have fallen because succession plans have included the kids.

You are not immortal. You are not building an empire so that future generations can live off your sweat.

But Look What You Have Achieved!

Life gives us about 40 years to play in the business world. For some, it is a period of struggle and subservience. For the entrepreneur, it is a period of opportunity where luck is what you make it. It is a game of chance where the successful stack the deck in their favor. You have played the game and won. The price to play was costly, in money, time, health, and personal relationships stretched to the breaking point, but that's history.

Today you have earned the right to revel in the glory of it all. You've proven yourself to yourself, your family, friends, and associates. What else can really matter?

This Is How It Works in Real Life

I have always felt (and still do) that business is personal. It's an important part of me. The successes and the hiccups are mine. My business often defined me. My entrepreneurial career has lasted 40+ years, and, with each new business I started, I thrived on the excitement and challenges.

I believed in setting my goals and expectations high and was hesitant to lower the bar, ever.

I have also learned that entrepreneurship can demand personal sacrifice. On one occasion, in the midst of selling one of my businesses, a venture which had consumed my time and attention for 5 years, I was offered a fair price and another pot of gold if I stayed on, or I could leave now.

That same morning I had gone in to my kids' bedrooms to kiss them goodbye and was overwhelmed with how much they had grown. When did that happen, and where was I?

And so I put greed aside and resigned that very morning. I wanted to spend more time with the family. For the first time, I came to the realization that retirement was more than a cliché. It was the best decision I have ever made.

Do what drives you.

CHAPTER 21

More Business Adventures of How It Works in Real Life

You just have to trust your own madness.

Clive Barker

Life teaches us "stuff." First-hand business experiences, adventures, and misadventures have always had a profound impact on me. These are worth sharing. There's a lesson to be learned from each one.

Flexible Ethics Has Its Limits

A large pharmaceutical company produced a laboratory reagent that sold for $10. It was packaged in a little nondescript brown bottle. Quite by accident, it was discovered that the reagent slightly diminished the resting tremor associated with Parkinson's disease. Overnight, the same product, same sized little bottle (with a new label, though) started selling for $995. Also, overnight, I abandoned the client. For me, it was flexible ethics overreach.

Be Nice to Dreamers

I was approached by an inventor who came across as the stereotypical absent-minded professor. Marching into my office with plans and drawings clutched under his arm, his vision was to build a high-speed railway running along the surface of the ocean between New York and London.

When I queried him about marine traffic, his response was that the line would be controlled by "Apple computers" that would temporarily drop the rail line well below the surface to allow for traffic. He already had a quote from a steel fabricator for close to $1 billion for the railing. I did not want to disillusion him. So when he asked me the cost to do a Business Plan, I quoted a ludicrous $475,000. He was delighted and said he would return when the funds were raised. I would have liked to meet up with him again. It was not my place to dispel his dream.

My Intimidating Office

In hindsight, I suppose that this was my experiment in an "ivory tower" business setting. My office was a corner suite with floor to ceiling windows on the 36th floor of a prestigious high rise. It was huge and intentionally designed to impress and, yes, intimidate. I placed my oversized desk as far from the door as possible so that visitors had to walk for 3–5 seconds to reach me. It definitely intimidated. I had learned that trick at my first job. When I met my first boss, I was escorted into his massive office and he had a boardroom table as a desk. When our meeting was done, he came to see me out, and I realized that he was quite short. His office setting was designed to compensate for his small stature and to feed his Napoleonic complex too. It worked for him, and an intimidating office also worked for me.

You Get What You Pay for

One of my early clients was an assembler of computers. Back then, the principal source of motherboards was China. My client established a supply chain with a Chinese supplier. He actually never met him, dealing via only written orders, faxes, and wire transfers.

At every opportunity, my client bargained with the Chinese supplier to reduce his costs. The supplier never said "no." However, my client could not help but notice that with each price reduction, the components and construction were growing cheaper too.

With his last order, my client received motherboards with paper thin wafer boards and no terminal connectors. Just dangling wires. Technically, the boards worked, but they were not useable.

My client learned his lesson. He traveled to China and built a stronger relationship with the key supplier. It was built on respect as well, that is, Guan Xi, respect for the needs of both parties.

How Much Will I Earn?

My team of consultants were primarily selected from a well-known university renowned for its MBA program. They felt entitled. It was likely part of their training, including shaking hands 101 and compensation discussions 200. It became annoying to glean through the talent when their primary focus was salaries, benefits, bonuses, and profit sharing. Imagine, profit sharing before they had worked even one day at our company! I devised a test to determine which were serious and which were tire kickers. I outlined the parameters of a prospective client requiring a Business Plan for investors. Here are the facts, give me a 20-page briefing paper. Those who refused were immediately discarded. Those who completed the task entered the hiring competition. The caliber of our team noticeably improved.

End Run on a Small Scale

My gardener was a young guy who did independent yard work. He was good, but remarkably unreliable. One day, he brought along his brother and left him in charge while my guy went off on one of his unlimited "emergencies."

The brother not only proved to be exceptionally reliable, but offered his services directly. "Don't call my brother. I can do it all. If you need work done, call me." It was an end run.

Obviously, even on small-scale relationships, flexible ethics are alive and well.

Give of Yourself, but Choose Your Charity

I was asked to sit on the board of an organization raising funds for sick and terminally ill kids. I saw it as giving back to the community and devoting some of my time and network to a worthwhile cause. We raised a great deal of money. However, at each board meeting, the chairperson arranged for several of the sick children to join us, tell their stories, and circulate. I argued that as touching as her intentions were, we certainly did not need that extra motivation. I already understood the value of the cause and the payback to the community. I could not sleep for several nights after each board meeting. I was haunted by the faces of the poor sick children. So I quit the board to preserve my sanity. It's okay to give back, and it is righteous to do so. It's not okay to be force-fed, whether it be guilt, compassion, or anguish, and it certainly didn't improve my eagerness to help.

Save Your Money, Do Your Homework

A major ice-cream chain who had recently entered the Russian market (Moscow) was flailing. Sales were dismal. Lots of lookers, but few buyers. I was asked to investigate and help determine the cause, and suggest remedial strategies. I analyzed the outlet, and I joyfully had to eat a ton of ice cream during my investigation. It wasn't as pleasant as it sounds. I counted foot traffic in the region. The location was good. The brand was well presented. The product was great. However, as I very quickly realized, at $5 a scoop, they were asking consumers to spend close to a month's wages on one treat. Hadn't anyone done any serious homework on the marketplace, demographics, spending habits? No. In typical arrogant fashion, they assumed "build it and they will come." They did not. The chain withdrew from this marketplace that was incompatible with their products. It was unfixable. That was my advice.

Don't Gamble on Fads

A client came to me with a plan to build a franchise of vaping shops. I was certain that this was a fad. Government regulations were already being drafted to control vaping, and certain lines of product were being banned. The client, however, was adamant. Based on his proposed capital expansion, I produced an analysis of how much money he would likely lose when the trend turned into a highly regulated fad. He backed away from the initiative and was grateful when the industry downturn hit, as I had predicted it would. Reverse psychology works!

A One-Hit Wonder

While I have had several amazing partners, I cannot end this chapter on adventures and misadventures without a story about partnerships gone bad. Let's call this particular partner "Johnny One Speed." In networking situations, he went for the jugular. He rarely listened but, instead, pitched madly. He had no patience for small talk, ever. When he pursued a client, he quoted high. It was as if every sale was to be his last, so "let's cash in." Instead of mentoring our young consultants, he preached, usually citing his own embellished successes. Once the money he had invested was spent, there was very little left that was endearing about him. The partnership honeymoon was over. It did not last much beyond his last investment check clearing.

Business Is an Adventure

There is little to compare to the exhilaration of entrepreneurship. The ebb and flow of business takes you on a journey from sweat-inducing roadblocks to mind-numbing highs. Ultimately, being in business is a privilege to cherish. It enrolls you into an academy of learning unlike any other, and leaves a residual plethora of stories to relate.

About the Author

A man wants to work for his pay. A man wants a place in the sun.
A man wants a gal, proud to say, that she'll become his loving wife.
He wants to give his kids a better life ... yes. Well hello, brother, hello.

Louis Armstrong, MCA Records

Jay J. Silverberg considers himself somewhat of a "Business Rebel." He has started and run a number of successful businesses. Jay has personally created enterprises in tourism, real estate, food, pharmaceuticals, consumer health care, resource development, and entertainment. His projects have spanned the globe, from North America to Asia.

As well, as an entrepreneurial trainer and business consultant, Jay has developed innovative programs for both the beginner and the advanced businessperson, from would-be entrepreneurs to those in full growth, acquisition, or asset divestiture. Mentoring has always been a cornerstone activity. Jay has delivered training and mentoring to thousands of entrepreneurs, managers, and business professionals.

His consulting practice, including a variety of clients ranging from start-ups and mezzanine growth companies right up to and including Fortune 500 firms, represented $1.5 billion in clients' capital projects.

Jay has also designed and created statistical predictive economic models that forecast changes to employment in communities undergoing material change. Further, these forecasting models help identify the wealth of communities. The economic planning tools are used extensively in government.

He has also represented government trade and economic development ministries at national and international conferences and has been instrumental in attracting foreign capital and partners to North America.

Jay has always been a believer in "real world roll up your sleeves" consulting and business development. This book is a culmination of his business adventures and misadventures and offers up a multitude of inestimably valuable lessons worth passing along. He hopes you enjoy this entrepreneurial trek that stands above and far apart from the sham "get rich quick" or humdrum "how to" business books, courses, and programs.

Jay resides on Vancouver Island in beautiful British Columbia, Canada, with his wonderful wife, Linda, who inspires him to always do better. Jay can be contacted at silverberg88@gmail.com.

A man's gotta do what a man's gotta do!

George Jetson (The Jetsons, 1962), paraphrased from John Steinbeck (The Grapes of Wrath), and further echoed by John Wayne, Van Heflin, and Charlton Heston

Index

OTHER TITLES IN THE ENTREPRENEURSHIP AND SMALL BUSINESS MANAGEMENT COLLECTION

Scott Shane, Case Western University, *Editor*

- *Dynastic Planning: A 7-Step Approach to Family Business Succession Planning and Related Conflict Management* by Walid S. Chiniara
- *From Starting Small to Winning Big: The Definitive Digital Marketing Guide For Startup Entrepreneurs* by Shishir Mishra
- *How to Succeed as a Solo Consultant: Breaking Out on Your Own* by Stephen D. Field
- *Small Business Management: A Road Map for Survival During Crisis* by Andreas Karaoulanis
- *Native American Entrepreneurs* by Ron P. Sheffield and J. Mark Munoz
- *The Entrepreneurial Adventure: Embracing Risk, Change, and Uncertainty* by David James and Oliver James
- *On All Cylinders, Second Edition: Succeeding as an Entrepreneur and a Leader* by Ron Robinson
- *Cultivating an Entrepreneurial Mindset* by Tamiko L. Cuellar
- *From Vision to Decision: A Self-Coaching Guide to Starting a New Business* by Dana K. Dwyer
- *Get on Board: Earning Your Ticket to a Corporate Board Seat* by Olga V. Mack
- *Department of Startup: Why Every Fortune 500 Should Have One* by Ivan Yong Wei Kit and Sam Lee
- *Family Business Governance: Increasing Business Effectiveness and Professionalism* by Keanon J. Alderson
- *Can You Run Your Business With Blood, Sweat, and Tears? Volume I: Blood* by Stephen Elkins-Jarrett and Nick Skinner
- *Can You Run Your Business With Blood, Sweat, and Tears? Volume II: Sweat* by Stephen Elkins-Jarrett and Nick Skiner
- *Can You Run Your Business With Blood, Sweat, and Tears? Volume III: Tears* by Stephen Elkins-Jarrett and Nick Skinner

Concise and Applied Business Books

The Collection listed above is one of 30 business subject collections that Business Expert Press has grown to make BEP a premiere publisher of print and digital books. Our concise and applied books are for...

- Professionals and Practitioners
- Faculty who adopt our books for courses
- Librarians who know that BEP's Digital Libraries are a unique way to offer students ebooks to download, not restricted with any digital rights management
- Executive Training Course Leaders
- Business Seminar Organizers

Business Expert Press books are for anyone who needs to dig deeper on business ideas, goals, and solutions to everyday problems. Whether one print book, one ebook, or buying a digital library of 110 ebooks, we remain the affordable and smart way to be business smart. For more information, please visit **www.businessexpertpress.com**, or contact **sales@businessexpertpress.com**.